NO
CHOIRBOY

MURDER, VIOLENCE, AND
TEENAGERS ON DEATH ROW

SUSAN KUKLIN

For Bailey, with love

SQUARE
FISH

An Imprint of Macmillan
175 Fifth Avenue
New York, NY 10010
macteenbooks.com

Square Fish books may be purchased for business or promotional use. For information
on bulk purchases, please contact the Macmillan Corporate and Premium Sales
Department at (800) 221-7945 x5442 or by e-mail at specialmarkets@macmillan.com.

Library of Congress Cataloging-in-Publication Data
Kuklin, Susan.
No choirboy : murder, violence, and teenagers on death row / Susan Kuklin.
p.   cm.
Includes bibliographical references and index.
ISBN 978-1-250-04445-7 (paperback) / ISBN 978-1-4668-5341-6 (e-book)
1. Capital punishment—United States.   2. Juvenile justice, Administration of—
United States.   3. Death row inmates—United States—Interviews.   4. Juvenile
delinquents—Legal status, laws, etc.—United States.   I. Title.
HV8699.U5K84 2008   364.66092'273—dc22   2007046940

Originally published in the United States by Henry Holt and Company
First Square Fish Edition: 2014
Square Fish logo designed by Filomena Tuosto

10 9 8 7 6 5 4 3

AR: 5.2 / LEXILE: 690L

CONTENTS

"Are you the sum total of your worst acts?"
                                    —Bryan Stevenson

CHAPTER ONE

I Was a Teenager on Death Row

DECATUR, ALABAMA,
AUGUST 12, 1993

Kevin Gardner was not home, even though it was way past his eleven-o'clock curfew. Kevin was a good kid, and it was unusual for him to stay out late without calling to let his parents know where he was. When he didn't show up the next morning, his father called the police.

That same night a police officer had received a dispatch to meet some individuals at Cedar Lake. They had discovered a body. It was Kevin's.

Before long, the focus of the investigation turned to Kevin's friend Roy Burgess Jr. Like Kevin, he was sixteen years old.

ROY: The judge said, "Stand up." I was crying bad. I was so nervous. "By the power invested in me by the State of Alabama, I hereby sentence you to die by electrocu—" He couldn't get the word out 'cause I went crying and screaming. In the court there was a big commotion. My mother. My father. My brothers. They was all screaming.

Nine or ten police rushed to the courtroom. There were two big redneck policemen—one had juice dripping down his chin from chewin' tobacco. They literally carried me from the courthouse through a catwalk, a tunnel, and straight down to the garage and into a squad car. There were a few ladies there, female judges. Their eyes were filled with tears. They tried to control it when I went by. They had their hands over their mouths, but I could see the tears in their eyes. The officer with the chewin' tobacco had a huge pistol, like a .357, some long-barrel revolver. He said, "You done killed one, but I'm going home tonight, and I'm going home alive." I was still crying. They sent somebody to gather up my property, what little I had. I didn't get to see my family or say good-bye or anything.

It's a big mess. A big mess.

They put me in belly chains and dragged me, still crying, to a squad car. We rode over five hours, maybe seven, to the state prison. They had the red and blue lights on, but no siren. They were going seventy, eighty. But for the time I came to this prison here—in '96—that was one time I was on the highway after the trial.

It was December, around seven or eight o'clock, so it was dark when we arrived. Before we even got there, I could see the prison for a mile or two. It was all lit up like a dome, like an aura. There was razor wire all around, and towers. My knees were knocking so bad.

I don't see myself as a monster, man. I can be productive. I can carry a job. I got a work permit when I was fifteen. My first job I worked at Popeyes. I cooked. The second job I had at Long John Silver's. And the third job I got at a steak house.

I got something to tell. I'm embarrassed to talk into this tape 'cause I know my grammar ain't so good. I'm into talking about this to you because I don't have many people to talk to here. The other inmates can be hateful. This place can make people hateful. There are some genuine gangsters here. I try to keep that in mind. I was a coward. I still am.

To get back to what happened when I went to death row, they searched me and took my measurements for clothes. They found out what I'm allergic to, if anything. They checked to see what I got that I ain't supposed to have. I just had my clothes, didn't have nothin' else with me.

Then I was taken to my cell. The cells were in tiers like you see in the movies. Twelve cells upstairs and twelve downstairs. They took me to cell 5-6. That's tier five, cell number six. It was tan, light brown, with steel walls. It got bars in the front of the cell. It was really small. It looked like a closet. Roaches everywhere. There was a steel cot with a mattress that they issue. I didn't get a pillow at first. There was a toilet and sink. There was a shelf over the bed for the TV, if you got one. Your family would have to buy it. The way I understand it, when a guy didn't have a family, other inmates would try to assist him, or the chaplain would.

The thing that tripped me out the most was after they had me processed. See, they took me to my cell. At that time you could have radios. Everybody was playing the blues. Soul music. It creeped me. There was blues all up and down the tiers. You know, I come to like it after a while, but back then it creeped me out so bad. On the street I listened to Led Zeppelin, Shardee, stuff like that. Everything but bluegrass. This was just the blues.

There were a few people there who I know'd from the county jail. They spoke to me when they saw me come in or heard me come in. Thank God I made it to my cell without cryin'.

I hadn't eaten all day. The guard went to the commissary and brought back a bag of cookies. I'm crying all night. Cryin' and eatin' cookies, all night long.

That first night, I thought the state was going to kill me right then and there. I'm thinking that I'd be dead in a month. I didn't understand what the appeals process was about. I thought I only had a few weeks.

Oh, man, I was scared. I had seen a lot of movies about prison, but I had never been to prison. And now here I am not only going to prison for the first time, but I'm going to death row, too. Man!

Roy's been in prison since he was sixteen years old. First he was in a county jail and then on death row in a state penitentiary. In 2001, his death sentence was reversed, and he was shifted from death row to a general, maximum-security prison. It's only been a few years since he's been off the row. This year is his tenth year locked up, an anniversary that weighs on him.

The time I was on death row I was a kid, man. I wasn't even able to vote for the politicians who opposed the

Donaldson Prison

death penalty. I wasn't able to join the military. I wasn't old enough to buy liquor. How do you sentence somebody that young to death?

As long as you're alive and breathing, you got a chance. Once they kill you and bury you, it's over. I got hope, but I ask myself how long is it gonna take? Ten years? Twenty? I'm twenty-six. In twenty years, I'm forty-six. Whew. Can't get that time back.

It's a mess. One big mess. I mean, the whole thing happened so fast. You don't take time to care about it. At least I didn't. I know I did an awful thing. If they change me from life-without to just life, the minimum time is seven. Seven years. That's if the family, the Gardners, don't protest.

This Friday will be August 13, and I will be off the street ten years. Man. I ain't seen the moon or the stars in ten years. I ain't felt grass on my feet in ten years. Women talk about a biological clock, right? I feel like I have a biological clock. I want a family. I want kids.

Man. *My whole life, man.* I'm done. Man!

Here's what led up to Roy landing on death row.

He was hanging out with a group of guys—Kevin M., Demetrus S., and Richie J.—who shared an apartment across the street from Roy's girlfriend's house. They were a few years older than Roy. No one can figure out how these guys paid their rent because only one of them worked, part time, delivering pizza.

"See, that's what I don't like about this whole mess." Roy leans forward. "They weren't what I thought they was at the time. They was gang members. I got very little respect for gang members. They were older. The one time I hung out with a tough crowd, it got me in trouble."

Roy lived with his family in a middle-class development. His mother worked in a bank. His father worked for an antifreeze company. Though he came from a stable home, Roy had his problems. He was in and out of school. "I want to tell you about that," Roy says. "I was just weak, just coasting through life. Man! I don't even know how to describe myself.

"I went to school. I was in the tenth grade when I got locked up, getting ready to go to the eleventh. I had teachers I admired, but I didn't pay them no mind at the time, you know what I'm saying? As far as teachers, man, I had three teachers I wish I could get in touch with now, just to let them know they made some type of impact on me.

"That's another thing—I had conflicts sometimes. I can't resist *conflicts. Sometimes I bite my tongue about this. I got in trouble a lot. But it was all kid stuff. It wasn't violent. Firecrackers to school. Pranks. I was suspended for saying certain things."*

What things?

"Saying stuff in class." [PAUSE] *"Sometimes we all need to grow up. But I never got suspended for fighting or things like that. There was a lot of self-deprecation 'cause I tried to fit in. I was a fair student, Bs, Cs, an occasional A. I liked science. Math intimidated me. The more I do math, the more beauty I see in it. I wish I had applied myself more."*

According to the trial records, Roy had been picked up for petty thefts, but he had no significant prior criminal activities.

"I was an ass."

Roy sips his Coke. His thoughts are beyond this room, in some other place. The small space where we are talking is quiet but for the humming of the air conditioner.

On the day of Kevin Gardner's murder, all the guys were hanging out at the apartment, drinking beer, smoking weed. They got to talking about how they needed some money. One of them said, "Let's go steal a car, or a car stereo, or something at the mall." They all hustled over to the mall. While the others went inside, Roy hung around the parking lot talking to someone in a white, sporty-looking pickup truck.

Roy hitched a ride from one end of the parking lot to the other with the driver of the truck. Later, at the trial, the man told the court that Roy stopped him outside the mall and asked for a ride, asked about his speaker system, asked if he had any money and did he want to buy a gun. The prosecutors used this to suggest that Roy was trying to carjack the truck. It had nothing to do with Kevin Gardner. According to Roy, what he was trying to do was sell the man a broken-down pistol.

After not coming up with money at the mall, Roy and his friends went back to their homes. Later in the day, Roy returned to the guys' apartment and asked Richie and Demetrus if they wanted to go to a party at Cedar Lake. Kevin Gardner, a kid in his class, was waiting to drive them in his blue Firebird.

Roy introduced everyone and climbed into the front seat. Richie sat in the back behind Kevin. Demetrus sat behind Roy.

The stereo was blasting so loud, Richie and Demetrus later said, they couldn't hear the conversation in the front. The car turned onto an unpaved road in an isolated area. Kevin refused to drive farther. They would have to get out and walk. According to Demetrus, Roy opened the door, then quickly turned and shot Kevin in the head.

"Oh, shit."

Richie and Demetrus said they were terrified about what had happened. They were scared and huddled in the back seat. They wouldn't help move the body. Roy had to do it himself. Then he drove the car back to town.

They returned to the apartment to find more guys. When told what had just happened, the new guys later described themselves as shocked and scared. But somehow they all had enough courage to come up with a plan to sell Kevin's car to a chop shop in Birmingham, a little south of Decatur. Roy and Kevin M. drove Kevin's car, and the rest followed in the car of a kid named Hayes.

As they caravanned to Birmingham, Roy and Kevin M. threw out items belonging to Kevin. A set of drums was tossed out on the road. *Golf clubs he had borrowed from a friend were left at a service station. In Birmingham, they couldn't find a chop shop, so they ended up leaving the car in the parking lot of a go-go club and returned to Decatur.*

Demetrus and Richie kept the car speakers. Roy went home with some CDs and the CD player. He later sold them to a former neighbor, who would testify at the trial.

Demetrus also testified against Roy at the trial. He told the jury that he could not stop thinking about the murder. He said that he had trouble sleeping. He described the following day, when all three roommates paid a visit to Demetrus's grandmother, who lived in the Cedar Lake area. First, they stopped to see if Kevin's body was still there. It was. They called the police and said they found a dead body while they were out picking blackberries. On the witness stand, but for a few minor discrepancies, the other two roommates told similar stories.

After the police found Kevin's body, they interviewed the three blackberry pickers. There was not much to go on, no obvious leads. One of the police officers had worked in narcotics divisions and already knew one of the guys. Since he knew where to find him if he needed more information, the police let Demetrus, Richie, and Kevin M. go home. Since they were all together in one apartment while Roy was alone at his family's home, there was plenty of time for the three roommates to come up with a single story.

Soon thereafter, the police brought the three guys back to the station house and started to interrogate them. By law they could be charged with the murder because they were accomplices. There was plenty of evidence that they took part in the planning of the crime and stole Kevin's car stereo. But Kevin M., Demetrus S., and Richie J. were promised complete immunity as long as they were not

the ones who pulled the trigger. They fingered Roy for the murder of
Kevin Gardner, and in return they spent not one day in jail.
   Roy, smiling, continues.

A VERY STRICT FAMILY

We lived in a three-bedroom house. My mother and father
had a bedroom. Me and Jeremy had a bedroom. O'mar
and my baby brother, Daniel, had a third bedroom. You
see, I'm the oldest of four boys. We were all born two years
apart. We're all close and love each other dearly. They
accept my phone calls and write—not as much as I'd like.
They're cool.

   I was really hyper as a kid. I took hyperactivity medication into my early teens. I always had to learn the hard
way. *On everything.* I got a problem with discipline. I have a
temper. I couldn't take advice from anyone. I thought I
was the exception to the rule. I figured that even though
people fail when they do something their own way, not the
regular way, I'm going to be the one to succeed. I learned
it doesn't work that way, not at all.

   I come from a very strict family. I was raised in a Pente-
costal home. Religion was my mother's idea. My daddy followed her lead. My father is religious, but he ain't weird
like my mom. We said prayers at dinner. I went to church
every Sunday morning. I ain't had no choice. My parents
forced me to go. Here I am sixteen years old, and every
Friday night, every Sunday morning, every Sunday night,
I had to go to church. No parties. No movies. No choice.

Couldn't even play with a water gun, a BB gun. We couldn't listen to secular music. No dancing. I could have girlfriends, but I couldn't bring nobody to the house. I had one girlfriend in my life. I was sixteen, she was fourteen.

When I was younger, my mom praised me. Then, when I got older, things changed. She's stubborn. I'm stubborn. And we both want it our own way. There was lots of yelling, a lot of punishment. I got it the worst of all the boys. I would get sent to my room, no TV, no desserts, no phone, stuff like that. I had to stand outside in the cold or the heat. She beat me with brushes, hoses, switches, Western boots, shoes. What was going on between me and my mom affected everybody else.

My mother went inside my head, mostly because of that religion. That's another thing that's kinda got me. Most of what I've come to learn about the world was completely opposite from what my parents taught me. They had me believing that the world is fundamentally good and every now and then you run across a bad person. I don't necessarily believe that. I believe that the world is screwed up and the good people are the exception to the rule. It's more rare to find a decent person than it is somebody who's going to try to take something from you. That's probably 'cause I'm in here. When I was younger, I didn't think that way.

My girlfriend, Jackie, she was white. She was my only official girlfriend.

I met Jackie at a skating rink. My mother never would let me go to no skating rink nohow—I lied, saying I had to go to work. It felt good to lie. It felt like I had beaten her, you know what I'm saying?

A lot of the guys here, they laugh when I tell them I only had one girlfriend, especially since I was on death row and everything. I had no occasion to date a black woman. I never slept with a black woman. I wasn't cool. I hadn't done anything. The guys here, they laugh and say, "They're trying to kill you, and you didn't have a chance to do nothing."

ARRESTED

It was twelve or one o'clock that night, August 16, 1993. I remember my baby brother, Daniel, he looked out the window and said somebody was outside. So I peeked out the blinds and I saw two police cars. I went to the front door and opened the latch a crack. Then I closed it and done took the chain off. I knew what it was about. I had only a pair of shorts on, and I wanted to put some clothes on. But my brother opened the door, and before I could get dressed, the police came in and said I was under arrest for murder.

After they told me that, my mother and father came to the door. My daddy, he got mad. That's the first time I heard my daddy cuss. He said, "Hey, get out of my house." I don't want to say the words he used, but you know what they are, right?

They said, "We're arresting your son for murder, man."

My mother screamed and fainted against the wall. They twisted me out of the house. I was still in my shorts.

We were on the street. There were at least five more

police cars. We lived in a predominantly white neighborhood. We usually stayed by ourselves. Everyone was up. Everyone was coming out on the street.

They read me no rights. They did that later at the police station. At the station, I could hear my mother and father screaming they wanted to see me.

I don't remember all the things they did when I was arrested. I know they photographed me and everything. They put me in an office in the detective division. I remember my daddy arrived and was yelling out front. I didn't want to see him. But the officers said I should have my daddy present when I give my testimony.

My mom stood by me, but not like my father. He loved me. *Me.* No matter what. If there is such a thing as unconditional love, a God, he most closely represents that. My whole life, I remember him getting up, going to work, coming home, sitting down to watch the game. Come back home and take a little nap. I mean, that's what he did. My old man didn't drink, didn't smoke, didn't run around the streets. My folks are divorced now. I was a contributing factor.

After Roy was advised of his rights, the state's brief reports, he admitted that he shot Kevin Gardner. Then he was put in a cell, alone.

COUNTY JAIL

It was a requirement that I had an attorney. He interviewed me. I guess he had in mind I was guilty from the get-go and it was an open-and-shut case, or whatever. He did just what he had to do to get by and no more. Since it was a capital murder case, there was no plea bargaining. There was no bail. At first I thought I'd go to juvenile, but they denied that. Gee-z-z-z-z-z.

There's a lot of complications involved with what went down, who was telling the truth and who was lying. Those guys, my friends, they weren't what they seemed. I mean, so many lies being told, so many thoughts being put out. The other guys never spent a day in jail. I was tried as an adult. I learned a lot over the years. I'm still learning.

During the time before the trial, I stayed by myself in the jail. I was treated good. I had the run of that jail 'cause I was absolutely the youngest person there. If I had seizures—sometimes I had these seizures, see, it's no big deal—I went to the hospital with no handcuffs, no nothing.

I took courses with everybody else. I took the tests and passed. Seventy-five percent don't. I do a lot of reading. It's a way to try to stay sane. Now I read classical literature—*Paradise Lost, Paradise Regained*. I read *The Divine Comedy* by Dante Alighieri. Some poems. Some Shakespeare. Man! I listen to National Public Radio a lot. They had this show on last weekend from a prison. They were staging Act V of *Hamlet*. That made me want to read that play so much. The guys acting in the play were actually convicted murderers. There is a lot of symbolism in that. I seen Mel Gibson's *Hamlet*— This is what I do *now*. Let me go back to *then*.

The sheriff—he died a few months ago—did the best

thing anyone ever did for me. When I passed my GED, he let me go to the graduation ceremony. Cap 'n' gown, suit and tie. No handcuffs, no shackles. He got my mom to buy two long-stem roses, one for my teacher and one for my girlfriend.

I was in the free world with regular people. He made the guards wear suits and ties like everybody else. That's the coolest thing anyone ever did for me *in my life*!

That sheriff, he caught hell doing what he did for me. "Why you let that murderer out?" Oh, he caught hell.

Later, I wrote him. I wrote him right before I got off death row. I told him that was the single most important thing anyone done for me. I appreciated him. I didn't expect him to do it. I said, "I appreciate everything you did. Even though I be on death row, I'll do whatever I can to better myself. And if you can't write back, I will understand."

While Roy takes another break, here's more about his trial.

THE TRIAL

The state's brief described the time when Roy took the stand on his own behalf. He admitted he was present when Kevin was killed but denied shooting him. He claimed that Demetrus shot Kevin from his position in the back seat on the right side of the car. He said he tried to warn Kevin that Demetrus and Richie intended to rob him. But Kevin Gardner, according to Roy, expressed no concern, no fear at all. Roy said he reluctantly took part in the trip to Birmingham

and that the others made fun of him because he was crying. He admitted to taking the CD player and some CDs from the victim's car. He also admitted to owning a gun. But the gun didn't work, so he sold it to someone he knew at church the Sunday following the murder.

What about that confession back when he was arrested? Roy told the court that he lied about shooting Gardner "so they would leave me alone." He felt that the police had already made up their minds that he pulled the trigger. He said he thought a confession was the best thing he could do to make it easy on himself.

Kevin M., one of the three roommates living in the apartment, testified that he heard one of the other two boys say, "Man, you can't just take the car from him. You have got to tie him up or kill him or do something." But they had full immunity and were not tried as accomplices.

The defense attorney put a young woman on the stand. She said she heard Demetrus and her sister arguing about something. She heard her sister say to Demetrus, "I know you are the one that shot Kevin." And then she heard Demetrus reply, "Yeah, I am the one that shot him, but you see who is taking the blame and you see who is walking free."

The sister testified immediately afterward. She backed up the previous testimony, that Demetrus had in fact admitted he was the one who had shot Gardner and that "Burgess was taking the blame." The defense then put up a third witness, Craig Turner, who testified that Demetrus had twice implied that "they got the wrong guy."

Roy in cap and gown (opposite)

No matter. Based on the testimony of the three roommates who had immunity, the jury found Roy guilty of capital murder.

Roy's ready to talk more.

Between my trial and the sentencing was thirty days. Besides my graduation, I never left the municipal prison. At the sentencing my mother, my father, and a lady who goes to our church all talked for me. My little brother was on the stand and spoke on my behalf. That brother of mine, he stood up in that courtroom and begged for my life. A little kid. I would say he was about ten then. But the judge knew that he was going to slaughter me anyway.

The jury came back ten against two in favor of life without parole. The judge overruled it and sentenced me to death.

I couldn't believe it. They had a conviction and a jury recommendation. Ten people out of twelve said I should get life without parole. Two people said I should be executed. I'm thinking they're going to give me life-without, right? Kevin's family was there. I wanted to talk to them. I . . . I want to . . . I just saw them that one time, at the trial. Even *they* say I got a raw deal. I wanted to tell them—whew! Hold on a minute. Hold on. If I— If I saw them again, I'd . . . I'd get on my knees and beg for forgiveness.

Roy leans way back in his chair. Way back. Twenty seconds. Thirty. Forty-five.

I mean, ten to two! I'm not mad at the judge. It gave me a chance to do a little growing before they threw me to the lions, here, in this place. Man!

LIFE ON DEATH ROW

Nobody's the same as they were when they first come to the row. They become different people. They are all better. Better people than when they first came to prison. Does that surprise you? I attribute it to reflection.

On the row, it's one man, one cell. On the row, they let you out of the cell two or three hours a day. At first I spent most of my time by myself. Then somebody brought their TV out of their cell. As I said before, we were allowed to have our own TVs. On the row, I'd watch TV and play Ping-Pong with the other guys.

The death row inmates loved me. They raised me. They taught me. They protected me. I was fortunate to have been around them. It was a buffer for me between coming off the street and later going into the general prison population. If I had gone right into general, I probably would have got raped or killed or went crazy. I don't know what I would have done.

I mean, at sixteen I was off the wall. I thought I had to be tough. These dudes, they were in their thirties, forties, fifties, sixties, and even seventies. They was twice my age. Some of them had been in prison, on death row, longer than I had been alive. They tolerated me instead of going

inside my head and choking the life out of me. They tolerated me, man.

They didn't take advantage of the weakness they knew
was there. You get a teenage kid coming in who knows
nothing about prison, nothing about people, nothing
about life, it would have been easy to take advantage of
him mentally, physically, even sexually. But they didn't do
that. They became almost like fathers in a weird kinda
way. They put up with my dumb questions, tantrums,
mood swings. They were nice and kind and understanding in spite of them having their own heavy burdens.
They educated me. They counseled me. They even fed
me when I was hungry. I respect them for it. You see, I
coulda become a victim. But they didn't exploit me on
death row.

Here's an example. On the row, the guys sit down and
play poker sometimes. They would play for things you can
buy in the commissary. I wanted to learn how to play. I
wanted to take part in it. They wouldn't let me. They said
if you just sit down and play, we're going to kill you. So just
sit down and learn.

We'd be playing basketball and I'd elbow somebody.
They sat me down and said, "You don't elbow anybody."
They could have crushed me. They could have got rid of
me. They didn't.

See, it's weird, I see myself like you see a two- or
three-year-old kid with a terminal illness. Cancer, AIDS,
leukemia, something real serious. Those kids still go out
and play and laugh and joke 'cause they don't understand

how serious the end is. They don't have a point of reference to miss anything. They don't have no bills to pay. No wife. No kids. No house. None of that, you know? So adjusting was easier for me.

To grasp the full range of where I was happened later. The older I got, man, the more it hurt. I can't speak for nobody else but me. What I want is basic. I want what the average person takes for granted. I want to cut my own grass at my house. You know what I'm saying? I want to walk barefooted across my carpeted living room floor. One day I want a wife. I want kids.

It's night and day the way the guards treat death row inmates from the way they treat the general population. There was respect for death row inmates. I think *respect* is the wrong word, but they were careful with the things that they did, with the things that they said. The police down there on the row is a whole different breed, just like the convicts. They don't disrespect us. They let us do our time in the cell. They let us scream.

Yeah, scream. I'll tell you 'bout that.

While I was on the row, three people were executed. I knew personally EV, Brian, and Ed. For the first execution, I said to myself, I'm going to fall asleep. I'm going to sleep through it. They used to do it at twelve at night. By seven o'clock, eight o'clock, I was trying to sleep. What I didn't know was about an hour before the execution, the inmates, everybody on the tier, scream at the top of their lungs. They scream in protest. That's what I told you about earlier, 'bout how the guards respect us and let us scream. And off those hollow steel walls it's really loud.

When I woke up it sounded like a war zone. Not just our tier, but all the tiers. There were at least two hundred men screamin'. I woke up on all that noise.

By this time I'm not on tier five, I'm on eight. Eight-U. I'm upstairs. I got bars in front of the cell. There's a catwalk in front of my cell, and there's windows out of the hallway.

Man, from my cell I could see the ambulance. And I could see the hearse to take the dude away. I'm upstairs in my cell. I'm at the window just looking. It's nighttime. I could see the people walking out to their cars and whatnot after they witnessed the execution. They're walking and holding hands with each other and giggling and talking, like they were just out of a movie or something. That just burns in my mind. It was like four or five people. They were laughing with each other.

Then you got the damn generator, a diesel generator. They turned it on every other day, and you know it is specifically for the electric chair. You can see it sitting in the yard, the black smoke, and the lights might flutter. They're practicing. And we watch.

Some guards say they would not take part in the execution squad. Some of them say it's just part of the job and they got to do it. Some of them say they don't mind pulling the switch one bit.

I don't like the death penalty for anybody. Because, like, three months ago they executed a dude named Tommy

Fortenberry. And then Keith Johnson got it. I mean whatever they did to wind up on death row, they did it. I mean, the specific act that they committed, that can't be taken back. Right? But they wasn't monsters. You can't just throw a person away. You know what I'm saying?

I can see it from the prison standard. You got a guy who hates the world, who's going to kill again and again and again, that's one thing. But if the person is willing to change or tries to do something with his life or tries to give back to society, you can't just slaughter people like that. Can you?

What's the purpose of the death penalty? Is it for prevention? Is it something to protect society? Or is it strictly for punishment? Vengeance?

If it's for prevention, then somebody on death row who's become blind or an amputee, then you should let them out 'cause they aren't capable of hurting nobody else. They just executed a man seventy-something years old. His name was JB. I knew him when I was on the row. He was a freak, man, a lovable freak. He loved sex. That's all he wanted to talk about. And he was seventy! Man! What can he do at seventy?

I was on the row from 1994 to 2001. During that time I met Bryan.

Attorney Bryan Stevenson took over Roy's appeal. He says, "Obviously the first challenge was to get him off death row. It was an unfair judgment, especially since they never prosecuted those other guys. The prosecutor used Roy's hanging out at the mall as evidence of guilt."

Bryan was cool. He made me feel comfortable. He gave me some hope. *Whew.* He used to send me stuff to read, stuff he thought would broaden my horizons. I'm better off for having met him, not just because he helped me with my situation, but because of my personal life.

We don't talk every day, but the key conversations we have had stuck with me. Aaryn *[Aaryn Urell, another attorney]* works with him. She cool. We write sometimes. There's another guy, I think his name is Jim, he used to come and see me. We had some pretty good conversations. Man! Sometimes I can't stand it. Sometimes, when I'm in the presence of certain people, I can't talk. Not because they are ignorant but because *I'm* ignorant.

The Alabama Supreme Court reversed the trial judge's decision and commuted Roy's death sentence. Now Roy faced a new hurdle, life without parole with the general population of a maximum-security state prison. This is where Roy lives now, possibly for the rest of his life.

To prepare for life with the general population, Bryan Stevenson knew that Roy would need help. Bryan says, "A lot of our conversations were about 'No, you can't do that,' 'Yes, you can do that,' 'You gotta think about this.'"

Bryan gave Roy projects: "You say you want to write? Why don't you write a short story? Why don't you write a song?"

He bought Roy books, lots and lots of books. He bought a screenwriters' guide. Roy was a good student. He was interested in learning. "He was into Shakespeare for a little while," says Bryan. "He was just excited to learn."

LIFE WITHOUT PAROLE

ROY: As best as I understand it, they took me off death row because something about considering my juvenile record and sentencing. My sentence was overturned to life without parole.

You get really demonized during these trials. You are categorized as someone worthless, just pure evil. You are vilified to the point where you question your own decency. Then, if someone connects to you and says, "You are a decent person, you made a mistake and you have to deal with it, but you are a good person, a decent person" . . . you grow. You develop. You change. You mature. At least that's what happened to me when I met Bryan.

BRYAN: And he was wonderful. He was talented and incredibly engaged by these writing projects, by these reading projects. That's what's so remarkable about kids. They grow up. The person you represent in the beginning is very different than the person you are representing a year later. Two years later. Three years later. Each time it is a different person, more so than with adults. These changes are profound.

Roy began writing poetry:

THE AGONY OF *IF*
If is a word I have learned to despise.
If is a word that brings tears to my eyes.
Trapped within the walls of this cold stone cell

I relive my past and on it I dwell.

I wrestle alone with *if* night and day

Wanting to change the past but finding no way.

In the past *if* loved me and helped with my plans

now it only mocks as life slips from my hands.

In youth if I had been wiser instead of such a fool

I could have harnessed *if* and used it as a tool.

If only I had lived a better life back then

I wouldn't be praying now for the mercy of men.

Yes, *if* is a word I wish I could forget

Since it only reminds me of all that I regret.

The move from death row to the general population was more diffi-cult than one would suspect.

ROY: I got spoiled on death row. I had done most of my time in a one-man cell. I had my own television. I watched educational stuff like *Frontline*. I really got into it. There's nothing here. No word processing. No typewriters. No tape recorder. We got nothin'.

BRYAN: He thought he had to show everybody that he was tough and strong. When threatened, he'd threaten back. Since he was still young, he had less skill and less ability to identify who in the prison population was ill, mentally ill. He couldn't distinguish between the inmates who were not really responsible for what they were saying and doing and those who were just trying to pro-voke him.

ROY: People tend to think I'm mean 'cause I got this frown. There's some people back there who I can fool 'cause I have this look, man. I sit on the bench by myself and frown at everyone and everything. It got to the point where it wasn't necessarily intentional. I got a lot of them fooled.

Then there are the inmates who consider me a nerd. Church boy. Square. A nerd in here? *Ha!* That's anybody who enjoys reading books. I thought I was normal, as far as the things I like to do.

BRYAN: In *[the general]* prison you've got people with all kinds of issues. The enemy is a rival gang. The enemy is not being able to get drugs. In a lot of ways, they are still living out the lives that brought them to prison in the first place—except that they are in a more desperate, violent, constrained environment.

Death row is different. There is a sense of community because they are literally condemned prisoners. Everybody has the same sentence. Everybody is facing the same fate. On death row you know what the enemy is—the enemy is the sentence of death.

On death row you are locked in a single cell. You are not exposed to other prisoners. You are locked down twenty-two, twenty-three hours a day. You're shielded from the dangers of prison life in the general population. Since you're isolated, you don't have to deal with the random violence and the recklessness that takes place in the general population. There are a large number of people who are emotionally disturbed and mentally ill in both places, but on the row they are locked in. If you're in a dorm with fifty other guys, and ten or twenty percent of them are psychotic, some violently psychotic, this is a very difficult business.

Now there are the obvious hazards of being on death row, which you are not shielded from. If you survive the death sentence, the hazards of being on death row seem a lot less threatening. But, of course, as you move toward your execution, this becomes less true. At that time you'd much rather be in the general population.

ROY: I like getting together with Bryan. We talk about my case, sure, but we also talk about philosophy and ideas. Bryan gives me a chance to understand who people are in prison. For the most part, it's all about day-to-day survival. I'm trying to figure out what's the purpose of all this. What is it all about, man?

When I was a kid, my parents told me that the love of money was the root of all evil. But over the years—me doing my own observing and coming to my own conclusions—to me the greatest evil in the whole universe is ignorance. Because a lot of times things would not have happened, or could not have happened, if more knowledge was involved. Ignorance, man.

Bryan teaches a college class, a law class. Man, I would love to sit in a college class. I should have been in a college class.

CALL ME ROW

A person come to death row for the first time, they scared. After they've been there for a while, the situation changes. You get used to it. You get everything delivered to you. There's a mailbox at your door. There's a laundry box at your door. You make no choices whatsoever. You don't have to be responsible for nothin', not when you're locked up.

It's different in here in general, different from the row. You have a little more freedom. That's not always so good. There are legitimately, seriously mentally ill people here. And then there's people pretending to be mentally ill. And then there are just straight bulldog monsters. And then there's people just doing their time till they can go home.

I'm still realizing something, and I'm putting it into play as much as I can. The best way to avoid any type of conflict is not to associate with anybody in the first place. Just avoid people as much as you possibly can. Keep out of trouble.

Man, see, a lot of these problems other guys have, I don't worry about because I was on death row. *"He was on death row so you better keep a long way away."* Ha! So I play it up sometimes. I have to. That's my nickname, Death Row. Sometimes they call me Row.

See, the difference is on death row you might know people for five, ten, fifteen years, so you become like a little family. You even get to know some of the guys' families.

But here in the population, it's so cutthroat. You might

be around a guy for two weeks and then they transfer him. It's constantly changing, so there ain't no loyalty. No loyalty. No respect. In the general population, everybody that can betray you eventually will. Do unto others *before* they do unto you.

This is the front of the prison. Going back there is like walking into a pigsty. When I reach the threshold of that main hallway, the air quality goes down, the temperature goes up ten or fifteen degrees. It stinks real bad. I'm in stink all day long.

There are roaches and water bugs and mosquitoes with feathers. And rats and mice that only eat the meat in the traps. I think they said the governor was going to walk through today so everyone is minding their Ps and Qs.

We eat dinner at about four or five. They turn off the lights at eleven, but we got a little night-light for reading. We shower every other day unless a visitor is coming. Then we get another shower. On the weekends the lights stay on till twelve. It's never quiet.

They take the blankets up in the spring and summer months. We have two uniforms. We got a laundry bag. We get our own towels and soap and underwear. We get a new bar every two weeks. Toothpaste once a month. If you get sick or need the dentist, you have to pay three dollars.

Some inmates can go outside and cut grass or work in the office. They don't let lifers do anything. Life without parole? We're warehoused, man. Human cargo. Just stacked up waiting for the reaper. Life with parole opens

Family visit, Roy and his nephew

doors. If they offered me trade classes, I'd sign up for every one of them.

The only thing I look forward to is mail. If I don't get mail, it's downhill till tomorrow and I wait all over again. I got me subscriptions to magazines: *Scientific American, Discover.*

I got drunk twice on the street and once more here. I never smoked so much reefer as in here.

I don't get many visitors. It's a long way for my family to

travel. I saw Junior *[his brother Daniel]* and my nephew for the first time. Cool dude. I got a picture with him and everything.

Like I said, my parents are divorced now. It happened while I was on the row. But now that my mom has her new husband, she's turned her back on everything she once shoved down my throat. The dude she's married to completely changed her. She came to see me a few months ago. She had her fingernails painted. She was wearing makeup. My mother! This was the first time *in my life* I had ever seen her with makeup on. She used to talk about other women wearing pants and stuff like they was dogs, you know? Now she's wearing pants.

Man! All those restrictions she put on me in my childhood. Making me go to church. I couldn't even play sports in school because it might interfere with church.

My girlfriend was married and is now divorced. She wrote me, telling me I was the only dude who respected her. I got to see her for the first time in twelve years. Afterwards, I wrote this poem for her:

THE BUTTERFLY (FOR JACKIE)
Today I saw a butterfly,
as we talked it just flew by.
When you saw it, it made you smile.
I wish it could've stayed awhile.
You said you loved them 'cause they're free
but something else occurred to me:

in my life I can't remember
seeing them out in December.
To me it was the strangest thing
seeing this little child of spring.
How could this beauty be so near,
facing the winter with no fear?
Could it be a sign from above,
that God himself blesses our love?
I can't say for sure how or why,
but today we saw a butterfly.

I'm fighting, man, 'cause I'm trying to stay as close to human as I can. I don't want to become a monster. I find more temptation to hate or just to be negative as the days go by. It's like you're carrying a tray of water for so long, eventually it's going to spill.

I just got out of solitary. I got into a fight with a guy in the cell. [SIGH] I don't make a habit of getting in other people's heads, but I don't like to see a group of people, or an individual, take advantage of anybody. There were two or three young prisoners here being trained. You know what I mean? You know. For sex and stuff.

I tried to tell 'em, "Look, man, they don't mean you no good. They got other things on their minds." Right? So word got back to the "trainers." They called me out. "Come in the cell, blah-de-blah-blah." When I went in the cell, before I closed the door, one guy done cut me with a razor. See, here inside my left arm. The police locked us both up. This is the first time I've had that.

■ ■ ■

I can't cry no more. I cannot cry. The only time I cried was
when my little brother got arrested a few years ago for
armed robbery. He was sitting in the car and somebody
went into the gas station store and robbed it. Everybody
got fifteen, twenty-five years. He got one-to-ten 'cause
he's a juvenile. He's still a teenager.

I want to cry, but I can't cry. I want to cry for the whole
mess. I want to cleanse myself. The tears won't come. It's
weird. When they do come, I don't think I'll have any control. But that's going to be good 'cause it's like having a
cold, and you've got to blow the germs out. I hope when it
happens it will be in front of someone who will give a
damn.

Have I learned anything? Truthfully? The name of the
game is this: Think before you act. Think about the consequences. My daddy used to say that all the time. "What
are you thinking? Think! Think before you act. You too
impulsive. You're too impatient."

I don't want to die in some prison cell. I want to see a
beach. I've been out of Alabama one time. I went to
Arkansas. I don't even count that as traveling. I was just
learning how to drive. I'm just sitting here. I don't have a
friend of my own.

Silence. Time ticks slowly, all is quiet. He looks up.

Can I hear my voice? I want to hear how I sound on the
tape.

Roy listens for a while, his arms crossed around his chest, swinging on the back two legs of his chair.

Do you think I can go back into society? I mean, if I get out someday, do you think I can make it in society?

In 2005, the Supreme Court declared the death sentence unconstitutional for juveniles, people under age eighteen. When Roy was given the death penalty, the best reduction available from an appellate court was life without parole. Now there is room to argue for a new trial. If his lawyers can remand Roy's case, he might be able to argue for a reduction to a straight life sentence. If this happens, Roy could be paroled in ten years or so.

Bryan Stevenson continues to challenge Roy's sentence.

CHAPTER TWO
The Fourteen-Year-Old Adult

Young people between the ages of ten and eighteen are usually tried in juvenile courts. But sometimes, if the crime is particularly violent, the prosecutor may ask the court to try the juvenile as an adult. In some states, fourteen-year-olds or older who commit murder, rape, or armed robbery are automatically tried in adult courts unless the judge turns them over to juvenile court.

MARK: I always have accepted responsibility. I've never put it off on anybody. I accept the fact that I'm going to pay the consequences for what I did. I killed a man. And my brother killed the man's wife.

I knew it was wrong. I knew it before it happened. I've had people telling me, "Oh, you didn't know no better, you were just fourteen. It was your brother leading you on." And even though that's true, in effect I'm the one that did it. And that's the bottom line.

I haven't had a day of peace since then. I don't enjoy

Self-portrait, by Mark Melvin (opposite)

life. I try to struggle through it. I got my little pain pills to deal with it. I call my artwork or my music my pain pills. They help me deal with, forget about, the situation for a while. In a way, I feel that I'm cursed and will be till the day I die. I know it's my fault I'm here. I did it.

My two oldest brothers, David and Richard, they were involved in stealing farm equipment and selling it to a deputy sheriff's father and mother. They had been doing this for a year before I caught on to what they was doing. Being fourteen, I was wild, and I wanted money, too. So I said, "Hey, let me go with you." I started going with them and stuff.

Well, the people they were dealing with, they got caught, and they were going to turn state's evidence and testify against my two older brothers. They weren't going to testify against me, although I didn't know it at the time. The investigator later told me they weren't going to because they didn't want to mess me up because I was so young. They knew I was pretty much riding with my brothers, trying to be like them.

My oldest brother, David, who's in prison on this case, too, he was a correction officer. He worked in the Florida prison system. He was my hero. I wanted to be like him. He had the perfect wife. He *had* stuff. He was respected. Everybody looked up to him. I didn't have a dad. David basically ran the family.

To make a long story short, David comes to me one day and tells me we're all going to prison. He had been telling me stories about prison, being that he works there and all. He said there ain't but one way to keep from going to prison. We had to keep those people from testifying. If they were killed, then they couldn't testify and we wouldn't go to prison. Well, I can't sit here and tell you I thought he was serious, because I didn't. I really didn't take it serious.

I had been in and out of juvenile. And now he's telling me we're going to prison. But the severity of what he was saying didn't click on me for real because it didn't seem real to me. I thought, Well, all right, okay.

One morning I was asleep and my brother woke me up. I had been out at my girlfriend's house the night before, partying, having fun, drinking. He woke me up and said, "This is what we've gotta do."

I basically said, "Okay," and I went with him.

I killed the man outside, and the wife was killed in the house. [PAUSE] You know what? I want to be honest. I still have to tell myself that I did it. I did it. Whether I'd do it today or not doesn't even matter. I did it then. It's been done. There's nothing I can do to change it.

I realized my life was over. I knew exactly what was going to happen. I knew I was going to prison. I knew in my heart. When the last shell was fired, I hit my knees to the ground. I knew I was done for.

I kept thinking, I just killed a man. And I was just as guilty of killing the wife, too, 'cause I was there. I wasn't actually in the house when it happened, but I was part of it. I had seen her after she was killed, but not before. No, that's not what went down. I had seen her *before* she was killed but not while she was being killed. I was outside the house.

Well, after the killing, I was pretty upset. It hit me so hard that I told myself if I don't get messed up on this I'm going to be a different person. It just really changed something inside me when it happened. I realized what I had did. I just knew that I went way too far. I set my mind that I was never going to break another law again, not stealing or anything.

Seeing the victims messed me up real bad. The only thing I wanted to do afterwards was get drunk. I wanted to get high, and I wanted to get drunk, and I wanted to forget about it. And that's what I set out to do. I tried to do it. I made up my mind right then, as soon as I got back to the house, I was through ever violating again.

My brother, he was acting like it was okay. There was actually another family member that had met us the night of the crime. I can't say who it was, but it was a very close family member who met us and helped destroy evidence.

For about the first four months after, it was hard. I had nightmares, even after I was locked up. I would wake up when I was in juvenile waiting to go to court—I stayed there about three weeks—I would wake up reliving what happened in my sleep. I'd wake up dreaming that I was still out there on the street. I was going home. Then I'd wake up staring at the wall. It affected me real bad. I come close to committing suicide. I wanted to. The police were watching me so hard that I couldn't. But I thought about it and really was serious when I was in juvenile.

Sometimes I would have problems dealing with what was real and what wasn't real. I had a lot of dreams, a lot of nightmares. Was the dream real? I was the only one locked up at the time. They hadn't locked my brother up at the time. He had just quit the correction facility.

THE ARREST

What happened was I had been called up for questioning, me and my brother both. And my mother. One of my brothers that was not involved in this case was involved in a theft ring. One day we went up to the county jail to bail him out. My whole family had come up. At the time the police had no clear evidence about the murders, no physical evidence, or ID, or nothing like that. The police were questioning Joseph, another brother. They were upstairs in the questioning room, and we were all downstairs in the parking lot. I saw Joseph peek out the window upstairs. He was up there with his daddy.

When I saw the investigators peek out, I knew that something wasn't right. I was actually fixin' to try to take off, but they caught up with me. They wouldn't give me a chance to get anywhere. I wasn't running—I was walking to the car.

I've been driving since I was about twelve years old, driving on dirt roads before then. I had a car, it was actually me and my mother's. A little Datsun. She actually had the keys in her pocket, and I thought they were still in the car. I tried to go, but I couldn't.

The police came over to me, and the first thing they said—and I'll never forget this—they said, "Mark Melvin, you're under arrest for murder."

I said, "Murder?" I mean, that was my response.

And my brother, my oldest brother, the one in prison now, said, "Just be strong." Basically what he's telling me is don't say anything.

They arrested me first. It was a couple of weeks before they arrested him. "Be strong—everything's going to be all right," he kept sayin'.

And I'm looking at him like a fool, like, Hey, man, they just charged me with murder.

From there I went through the booking process. They transferred me over to juvenile until I went to court for certification hearing to stand trial as an adult. My mom came to see me. I cried, "I wanna go home." What could I say? I mean, my life was over.

From that time forward, my brother tried to put the case off on me. He knew I loved his wife a lot. She was like a big sister to me. Her name was Pam, and she had had cancer and had surgery. They were trying to have children. She wasn't able to, but my brother told me that she had finally gotten pregnant. That wasn't true. He was telling me that because he knew I loved her, and he knew that I would probably confess to everything and take the full case on myself, just to spare her and him. They knew that he was involved, but they didn't have any evidence on him. I told one of my other brothers what really happened. And when he was questioned, he told the authorities that David did it. There were certain things about the scene that only the people who did it would know.

Once I found out he was trying to put everything off on me, and after talking to a few people in the county jail, older guys, I had come to the conclusion that I wasn't going to prison for two capital murder charges and let my brother laugh at me. I realized that apparently he wasn't for me like I thought he was, and I actually started to kinda hate him at the time. I don't hate him today, but at that time I did. I thought he was betraying me and using me. I was always taking responsibility for what I did. I always have. I'm not a Christian by form, but I do believe in spiritual law. I believe what you do is going to come back to you. It may not come back in the same form, but it's going to happen. I believe I'm paying, and I have paid, from that day forward. And my life's been miserable.

NEVER WAS A GOOD KID

You know, I never was a good kid. No, ma'am. I had problems. I had real bad mood swings. A lot of things I did, I didn't understand. Sometimes I would hit on my brothers and stuff—my younger brother, my older brothers. Didn't matter. I wanted to be grown up.

I believe I had serious problems, mental problems, I really do. Everybody thinks that they have some problems, but I remember laying outside on the front porch, and my mother was rocking me, and asking her, "Why you ever had me? What's wrong with me?" Because I would have these mood swings so bad. And I would have these feelings and I wouldn't understand why. It was actually a physical feeling where I would be literally pent up inside and I'd just blow, you know, even though this wasn't done in anger.

Who I was then, I'm not now.

I have five brothers, one sister—same mother, different fathers. We lived in Pensacola, Florida. Now they've moved around some.

Although Mark lived in Florida, the crime was committed in Baldwin County, Alabama. That's why he was tried and incarcerated in Alabama.

My father never was there. My mother, she did the best she could, but she didn't have much education. She had seven children. She had her first child when she was sixteen. We were always on welfare, a real poor family. She did the best that she could. But it's hard to raise a bunch of boys by yourself. Once they get that age when you can't really tell them nothing, and there's not that male figure to add strength to it, basically they just do what they want to do.

I always wanted to make money. I always wanted to work. Actually, I had gotten a legal job with my uncle on a construction crew. I wanted to be successful. I wanted to do good. That's always been the thing driving me.

When I actually got that job, I was trying to grow up, not really knowing how. Who had I to look up to? My oldest brother? I thought he was good people. He handled his business well. But I grew up in a harsh environment, in and out of juvenile and stuff like that, so I was used to violence and stuff of that nature. Hustling and making it.

My mother had me locked up several times because she couldn't deal with me, or she didn't want to deal with me, I'm not sure which. I feel like she just did the best that she could and that's all I can really say about that. Because I can't second-guess what was in her mind at the time. I love my mother, and I respect her.

She never beat me. She never was a drug addict or an alcoholic or anything like that. She really did do the best that she could do. It was just too much for her. Once I had been locked up in juvenile, I started feeling like a castaway. Everybody was looking down on me. And I thought, Well, okay, if they're looking at me as this castaway, well, this is what I'm going to be. And I didn't have no problem doing that. It come natural, it come real easy to me.

Mostly there were some thefts, not going to school, things of that nature. There wasn't nothing serious. I stole a Ford one time, riding around in it. I was about twelve, thirteen. They actually locked me up one time on an assault, although I never did assault anyone. What happened was my mom talked to the counselors, trying to get me some counseling help, you know, some type of program or something. And they were telling my mom that the only way the court would do that was if I was locked up. Then I could go before the judge and he would sentence me to a program. So basically the assault thing was a way to get me locked up. Instead, it got me a record. So now it showed that I had an assault when I was a juvenile. I never did assault my mom. There was actually an assault between me and my stepfather, who was drunk.

I understand what she was doing. I can't say it was wrong, 'cause she was doing the best she could. She had no money to put me in a program. The state had to do it.

Like I said, my brother was a correction officer and he

had a .38. I've never been enthralled with guns. I couldn't tell a 9mm from a .38. I didn't have a lot of guns in my house, but I always hunted and stuff like that. I had two, three shotguns and a .22.

I never did have any desire to do violence or anything like that. I would lose my temper. I would go on those mood swings, and sometimes I would act out. But as far as just setting out to do violence, I was never like that. I never thought about being a bad person, or being a feared person. That came later. I had to become that to survive.

COUNTY JAIL

In the juvenile facility, they wouldn't cut my hair because they were scared. They musta thought I was gonna get 'em and stab 'em with the scissors 'cause I had just been charged with two murders. It made me feel so bad. It didn't make me feel cool or nothing like that. It made me feel real bad, I mean *real* bad. They hurt me bad. I couldn't be around other juveniles in the juvenile facility because of my case. I'm watching the other kids go out and play in the recreation area, and I was not allowed to. I was locked up in isolation. That affected me real bad.

Later on I could go out alone, but I was in handcuffs and shackles. They shackled my feet and handcuffed my hands in front of me. I was fourteen. They kept security on me so tight. I was in an isolation cell with the lights on all the time. Nothing in the cell except a toilet and a shower. Very little talking. I sat by myself.

The guards would come by and look in every once in a while, just to make sure I was alive. I wasn't scared. I was sad. I felt like an animal. That's how I was being treated. You go from being on the street one day, playing with your brothers and sister, and, you know, you're being loved. Then next day you go to an environment where an individual is scared even to be around you. It's not good.

I was shocked when I heard I was being tried as an adult. My attorney at the time gave me this rigamarole about what he thought was going to happen to me. He said it would probably be about three weeks before my certification hearing and that they were going to try me as an adult. He was actually a good attorney, but he used to be the DA in the same county. I didn't know it at the time. When I was at the county jail, I met a man who came from death row. His name was John. He told me about a lawyer, Bryan Stevenson, and how to make contact with him. And I did. He's been my lawyer and best friend ever since.

E-MAIL FROM BRYAN: We got involved in Mark's case before his plea. We'd heard that he was possibly looking at a plea for life without parole and we didn't think that made sense because he was not eligible for the death penalty. It did not make sense for him to plead to the maximum sentence. We wrote a lengthy document which sought to mitigate his crime and support a reduced sentence.

MARK: I never did go to trial. I ended up plea bargaining for life-and-ten sentence. And that's what I have. It's life with parole. I would have received life without parole if I didn't plead. I knew I couldn't get the death penalty. At the time, the William Thompson case had been settled by the Supreme Court. Thompson was a fifteen-year-old who had received the death penalty. The Supreme Court ruled he could not receive the death penalty unless he was sixteen years or over at the time the crime was committed. However, he could receive life without parole, and that's what he got. So me, at the time, I got the sense that the most I could receive was life without parole, and I pled out to life and ten. I thought, someday I may have the chance for parole.

DONALDSON STATE PRISON

I was moved into level six, high security. It was real scary. When I first got there, I was in lockdown. It was bad. It was like you see in the movies. It was big. What was so intimidating was the size of the cell blocks. To get to my cell I had to walk down this real long hall.

I was walking down this hall carrying my property and it was so quiet. My property consisted of my bedroll and bottles and writing materials and stuff like that. I was walking forever down this hall. Quiet. That's what threw me off. The quiet. It was around lunchtime, I guess, about eleven, twelve. But I keep seeing these little halls off to the side. They didn't look like they're really going anywhere. Anyway, we ended up turning into one of them. There were rows of cells with bunk beds. There were about four showers to a block of cells. It looked like I was in a big warehouse, a hangar, you know. I had never been around nothing like that before. It was lockdown.

It was so quiet. Okay, now, let's see, why is it this quiet? I asked myself. I had an idea what to expect because I had been in the county jail two years talking to people coming down from prison. But I never heard nothin' about the quiet.

The officers inventoried my property. We were going through the process when all of a sudden, I seen one head sticking out the door. And then I seen another. And then they started talking, and I seen all these heads in all the doors and windows. And they started hollering and whistling. It was like you see on TV.

"That's mine."

"Oh, he's fine."

"That's my boy, there."

I'm sixteen years old by now, and I'm thinking, Oh, my God, they're going to kill me. I put on my mean look. I was scared to death.

And the officer? He's just sitting there, laughing. Most of the officers there are not professional, not anymore. One time they may have been. But now it's not a professional job—it's more a labor job. They don't care. They really don't care. You have some that do, but they don't take an interest in your well-being for real.

They put me in a cell with a white guy like me, who actually helped to get me jumped on the next day. He said he did it 'cause he was scared of the black dudes. He was a whore. What I mean by that is he had a man, or men, that he would let have sex with him so everyone else would leave him alone. He was about twenty-eight, twenty-nine. He was grown.

Everybody was sending notes to me and stuff, wanting to know this and that. I'd flush them down the toilet without even reading them. I had never had anything like that. What was going through my mind was, Man, y'all are sick, you know what I'm saying?

The next morning, I come in off the wall and I'm sitting on a chair. I had one of my legs propped up on part of the wall with my arms crossed. A dude come up to me and said, "What you standing on the wall like that for? What's you in? A Disciple?"

The Disciples is a gang organization. I know nothing about no gangs. I had never been involved in anything like that. I said, "No, I'm Mark. I'm Mark. I know what the organization does, but I ain't got nothing to do with that. I don't know nothing about that."

"Well," he said, "you can take your foot down."

Now, I know I can't take my foot down because if I do, I'll just succumb to him, you know what I'm saying? And I would be in a lot of trouble. So I knew I had to stand my ground. I said, "I ain't moving my foot nowhere."

Another man from the same gang comes up and he says to me, "What you calling me a bitch for?" Excuse my language.

And I'm going, "I ain't never even spoke to you."

He said, "I know you told your cell partner that I was this and this." This is my second day, and I didn't even know these dudes.

I already knew the game. They didn't need no reason to come at me. They were just making an excuse, an opening line.

"Leave me alone."

Another man was coming up the stairs. I was on the top tier, and I tried to position myself because I knew they had a thing about throwing people off the tiers. I tried to position myself so I could keep everybody in front of me. Now there's three of them standing there in front of me and one more was coming up the stairs. The guy coming up the steps started playing a mind game. He says, "Y'all don't mess with him, that's my homey boy!"

Basically, he's trying to act like he was going to save me so I'm supposed to be indebted to him. He was actually their partner, but he was trying to run a game off me, like, Okay, I saved you from getting beat up so you're supposed to be appreciative toward me. It's just the games that they play.

I said, "No, I ain't your homeboy, I don't even know you. You can just go and play that with somebody else."

Well, that's when everybody jumped on me. And if it weren't for the officer who came up, I would have been hurt real serious.

Rape was my biggest fear in Donaldson. I mean, full-grown men who had no homosexual characteristics were raping men. They were like animals. I felt like I was living in a zoo and around a bunch of animals.

You see, in prison there's this mind thing. I mean you got your freaks that just want to have sex with you—and there's a lot of them. But most dudes, they want you to

break. They want you to get in compliance. They want
you to put on a skirt and panties and makeup. They
want you to fall in that role. And the one way they try to
get you to do that is to break your spirit, break you down
so you accept the role they want to put you in.

It isn't just jumping you or actually trying to rape you,
because that would probably be a one-time thing, and
that's not what they're about. It's trying to break you to
the point where you agree to do it. If they keep beating you up enough, you'll hook up with somebody that's
respected, be his boy, you know what I'm saying? That's
how this thing goes down. If they rape an individual, nine
times out of ten, if that individual don't want to be raped,
he's going to be hurt, and he's going to the hospital. Then
the rapist is going to be locked up. So the rape is a one-
time deal. And then the rapist has a rape case. Whereas if
you just beat him up again and again and again, what are
they going to do? Write you up for a fight? They tried a lot
of intimidation to break me down.

When I first got locked up, coming from the street, I
was not racist. Period. I didn't have no reason to be. But
in Donaldson it was "white boy this," "white boy that,"
everything that was said was "white boy." When you have
that projected on you for so long, then you have trouble
from inmates because you're a white dude, and you're so
outnumbered, you can't help but have some animosity
toward that race that's doing it to you. So I started to get
some racist views and stuff like that. I can't say it's racist

because I didn't look at a black man and say, "I don't like you because you're black." I ain't really care what color they was.

It just so happened that most of your young dudes were black. They were gang members. You had the Crips. The Disciples. The Bloods. El Rubens. I think the biggest gang environment would be the Disciples. They called themselves an "organization," but they were really just a gang. A man saw me fighting one day and saw that I wouldn't back down. He told me that he was a Crip and said, "I'm taking you down to Crips." But I wasn't interested. I never joined a gang.

There ain't too many white people in prison, period, especially in Alabama. It's a racist environment. The only thing you can do is be tolerated. If they know that you'll do something to them, they'll leave you alone. But as far as just liking you, there are very few. In Donaldson I never did have a friend. I never did have a partner. I never had anybody I trusted those three years.

I've seen people stabbed. I've seen people beat up. I've seen officers beat up. I think the worst thing that hurt me, or touched me, what made me realize where I was at, was when an old man about seventy years old fell down the steps. And when he fell, they would laugh. The whole dorm, laughing. Me, it brought tears to my eyes because this was an old man. And he was hurt. And it brought tears to my eyes, and I realized where the hell I am. Look where I'm at. That really was the biggest thing, other than getting into fights and stuff like that. That incident is what I remember most of all throughout the years, everybody laughing at him. There wasn't nothing, nowhere in the world, funny about that. I couldn't even think of something funny. It didn't even look funny.

I was back in lockup at that time. They knew I was a security risk because of my age, my looks. I was really young looking. I was real clean-cut. They knew I was a security risk. I could have been raped. By now I had already been beaten up by gang members. They kicked me, stomped me in the head. I was real lucky that I didn't get seriously hurt. If the situation had been just a little bit different, I would have been hurt bad. But I was always outside the cell. If they had got me in the cell, there's no doubt in my mind I would have been raped. That was their main motive, to catch me right inside where they could get me. And I knew that.

The officers would sometimes click open your lock so that the other inmates could run in the cell and stuff. Anytime the doors were opened, I was always the first one out the door. I had to get away from the cell because they weren't going to do anything out in the open.

I even booby-trapped my cell. I mean I booby-trapped my cell by putting stuff on the door, like water and shampoo and stuff like that, in case they ever did try to get in. It would trip them up a little bit and it'd give me enough time to wake up. That was like a nightly ritual. It was a very stressful time. My digestive system basically shut down on me. My stomach hurt so bad just from stress. I couldn't eat. I couldn't use the bathroom. It physically affected me bad, just being stressed out that much.

I had no problem with the officers. I was always respectful toward them. Because, number one, out of fear because they would jump on you. Those officers didn't play. They could hurt you.

I went to the captain and I asked him to place me in protective custody. He said, "No." He said, "You're going to have to grow up and be a man."

I said, "What you're telling me is that in order for me to be a man, I have to be gay, stab somebody, or be stabbed myself." And he shrugged his shoulders. He didn't say anything. I walked out of his office and I never asked another officer for help from that day forward.

I became a bit hard myself. I got a real bad attitude because I thought I'd be killed at any time. So I started getting that daredevil mentality and attitude where I'd start some things. If somebody looked at me crazy, I'd go off on them. I got an attitude.

That helped me. Once I started taking that position, instead of being a scared white boy, I became a crazy-ass white boy. That's what they called me, Crazy-Ass White Boy. "Don't mess with him, he's stupid." Not that they were scared. You're talking about people with life without parole. They don't need to plum anytime. They ain't scared about nobody. They don't care about you stabbing them or nothing else. They don't care. What do they got to lose?

It's easier to pick on somebody if you can get by with it. I just quit letting anybody get by with it. Off the top of my

head, I would say I was in about six *serious* fights. And
three of those were by gangs jumping me. There were
other not so serious altercations.

The last fight I had there, I had two teeth knocked out. I
had to have one broken off. And I got my head busted,
right here. That was the last fight I was in. I didn't get
new teeth. They told me I have to have five missing to get
new ones. I told them I don't care to get three more taken
out like these two. [LAUGHING]

In my last fight there, a man grabbed me and patted me
on the butt as I was walking by. I turned around and
slapped him. Since I had asked the captain for help and he
said he wouldn't give it, I was prepared to do what I had to
do. I even had an ice pick for protection.

In some prisons it's easier to get contraband than
others. Look at this rod on this cabinet right here. We
have them over in the trade school and the maintenance
department. It ain't nothing to cut a piece of it off and put
your point on it. Then you have an ice pick. Well, this ice
pick I got from an old white guy, an old convict who knew
what time it was. He had life without parole. He knew I
was in trouble 'cause I was mad at several people.

One morning I went on the walk and a couple partners
came over to me. They said, "Why are you over by the
fence here? Come back where we sit and deal with it.
What's you going to do? Get out? Catch out?"—"Catch
out" means, you know, run with the folks. "Hey, we here
and you need help."

Well, I knew what their help meant. I wasn't going to go

with them. I just had to swallow my fear and deal with it. When they came at me, I'm thinking, that one's got a knife and he's going to threaten to kill me. That's his MO. I reached down to get my ice pick and the man throws his hands up in the air. He doesn't have a knife, he just wants to fight.

And that's when it hit me. That's when I realized just how much time I got here. Till then, I'm thinking I just want to do good, get out, and go home. At that minute I thought, Look how much time I have to do.

I put my ice pick back in my boot, and we got in a fight. He got the best of it, and I was messed up real bad.

That's when I was transferred, because they didn't want us in the same institution. The man was an old convict who knew how to do time. He told the officer I had a knife on me, and they gave me ten years suspended sentence for it.

The judge himself looked at me and said, "If you're at Donaldson, I know you've got problems. I don't know why they sent you up here."

I was in Donaldson about two to two and a half, three years. I had been in the county jail two years prior to that. So, by now I had been locked up over four years.

HOLMAN CORRECTIONAL FACILITY

Holman's where they have the electric chair and everything. It's a scary place. But I was happy there. I was very pleased to be away from everything I had been through. You see, at Holman there's a lot of old-timers. That means less stupid, unnecessary trouble. Usually when there's trouble, it's serious, whereas in Donaldson it was chaotic twenty-four-seven. You got a bunch of kids up there at Donaldson. So I was glad to get away.

A man who was being transferred with me was saying, "Man, I don't know what we're going to do. We're going down a hole. They kill folks down there."

I said, "What you talking about? They killin' 'em in Donaldson, too, where we've just come from." I told him, "Man, I'm glad I'm going to Holman." Going through what I went through at Donaldson, I figured I could deal with anything, at any prison, anywhere. I done been through the worst. The only thing they could do is kill me so I was glad I was going down there. I was going to be closer to home. I thought maybe I'd be able to see my family. I hadn't seen them much at all. It turns out I seen my family only a couple of times at Holman. I got three visits the two and a half years I was at Holman.

From day one at Holman I didn't have any problems. I had three incidents with inmates confronting me on the homosexual level because I was skinny and clean-cut and everything. But once I dealt with that, I never did have any problems. At Holman the yards stay opened all day. You could basically stay out there all day, if you wanted. They had weights there and a basketball court.

We lived in blocks and bunks. It was all out in the open. We had this much room—the size of this table was the space between each bunk. Two beds a bunk. I'm not sure how it is now. They changed it.

They got you up around seven o'clock, and they cleaned the cells out. You take showers in the evening, around ten o'clock, unless you got a job in the kitchen or something. Then you can shower some other time.

We ate in a mess hall. I've been eating in prison so long, it really isn't bad. [LAUGHING] Prison food isn't so bad. They've had a lot of changes in the prison system through the years. The diets are not that bad. I mean they're not that great. The meat isn't that great, it's by-products. It's not that good for you, for real.

Five days out of the week, we get to have two biscuits, a scoop of eggs, grits, and jelly. That's the breakfast we have. We can get some juice, but it's really like watered-down Kool-Aid. Really, that's what it is. They've just started giving us cartons of milk now, which is something they had cut out years ago. So that's good.

For lunch we had the same five weekly menus. Mostly we had some rice and a meat patty. A roll. Sometimes a vegetable. Maybe some Jell-O or something like that. One day it may be some cookies. Sometimes they give us chili con corn, or whatever you call it. *Chili con carne.* It wasn't exactly tasty, but it's food and it's what I'm used to.

Dinner and lunch is basically the same type of meal. But every other Sunday we get chicken. Fried chicken. That's the best meal that we have.

You get a full meal. You don't go to bed hungry. You may not get all that you want to, but you're not going to go hungry.

They have canteens in all the prisons. Individuals can get money from the street, from home, and then they can go to the canteen and buy stuff. Sandwiches. Ice creams. Drinks. Stuff like that. It's nice to have.

It's like living in a ghetto. There was a lot of drugs. A lot of hustling. Home-made whiskey. A lot of gambling. A lot of homosexual activity. It's just like a small community.

Holman's got its own rules. It's got its own events that take place. The police didn't mess with you down there, at least they didn't at that time. I heard it's changed since then. They didn't get in your business as long as you didn't cause any problems. Their main concern was that you wasn't killing anybody.

They didn't like hard drugs in the prison, such as shooting dope, or cocaine, or crack, or anything like that. They didn't want that because inmates on it are going to cause trouble. Whereas a little reefer, or something, they just laid back and laughed. They didn't really harass anybody on stuff like that. Everyone was scoring drugs. Everyone was scoring the slick picks. Slick picks is the gambling, picking your football teams.

The officers basically let us run the prison. The individuals who ran the prison had earned enough respect that they set a standard. And people lived up to that standard 'cause if you didn't, you was an outcast. You couldn't get nothing done for yourself.

The standard was what they called the convict code. Stay out of folks' business, don't tell on nobody, don't disrespect anybody. If you do, you're going to be dealt with. It didn't matter who you are. You knew that if you dis-respected a man, if you stole something from that man, you're breaking the code. And if you do that, you were running the risk of getting hurt—very seriously hurt.

Like I said, there were very few fights down there at Holman. There wasn't much petty disrespect going on, so that made life easier. But there was always that potential for a serious eruption of violence.

There were two incidents while I was there, one right after another. One was a race riot. One was against the police. They stopped that before it happened, though. What happened was the police were too hard on us for no reason. You can't run a maximum-security prison with people with life without parole like they've got a ten-year sentence. You can't do it. This prison is their home. If you go violating a person's home, they're going to do some-thing back. Besides, they ain't got nothing to lose.

There was another race riot, which I was blessed to have missed. I had actually just come off from work. I had a job. I was working on maintenance, which I really enjoyed. It kept me busy. Prison maintenance. Upholding the prison. You know, plumbing, electrical stuff of that nature. I'll get to that later.

When I went to Holman, I had a real bad attitude. I was full of hatred toward everybody. When I was at Holman, that's when I really started growing up, as far as under-standing people, different types of people. I realized the white dudes were just as bad as the blacks. They would cross you out and cause you trouble just as much. So at first I became a loner, which is what I was at Donaldson, I was a loner. I was real antisocial. I didn't associate with nobody. There were very few people I talked to.

In time I was going to commit suicide. I made up my mind. Not my mind, my heart. I just got tired of living. Tired of being miserable. Common sense told me I would rather be dead and not feel nothing than be alive and be miserable and hurting.

I combed through the Bible. I don't remember what it was I read, but something helped me. The next morning, I woke up a different person, with a new sense of what's going on. I thought things could be better. I could make it. Life was worth living, no matter what.

I still had problems with the homosexual activity all around me and my spiritual beliefs. I had a big problem with that. I guess, in a way, I adapted my own religion around my own habits.

Basically my religion is don't be as big a dummy today as you was yesterday. Don't make the same mistakes. Try to learn from other people. Don't be judgmental toward people. Try to show some kindness to somebody that's hurting. And that's my religion.

I feel a lot kinder now. A lot. A lot. I mean before I wouldn't even speak to people. I started hanging around with people that were well respected in the prison community. They were the ones that basically ran the prison. I got in with them, and they liked me because I grow'd up real old for my age. They liked having me around.

I had two people I kinda listened to growing up in prison, a guy named Lee and a guy named Buddy. These two guys opened my eyes to a lot of stuff about prison and life in general.

Lee taught me a trade. He got me on the maintenance crew and taught me that. He taught me the leather trade, how to do leatherwork. He was a father figure to me. I got love for him till this day. He took an interest in me. He saved me. He was in prison for murder. He had the same sentence I had, life and ten.

His case was a very controversial case. He killed a man he knew who beat up an old woman. Lee took him out in the woods. He was basically just going to scare him and beat him up. But the man had a tire iron and hit Lee with it. And Lee shot him.

One time he escaped from Draper prison. Stayed out eight years. He was so successful in some town in Wisconsin. He was a construction worker. Everybody liked him. When he got caught, the folks in the town couldn't believe that he was an escaped convict. They put him on *The Oprah Winfrey Show*. That's where he met his wife. She was watching TV. And she married him.

Buddy was a little different. Buddy was the most feared man that's ever been in prison. He was a very big individual. He had been in prison for years. He grow'd up in prison, him and his brother both. And they were very respected individuals because of their violence, because of their leadership abilities. They were the dope men and the hustlers. They ran the prison.

When I met Buddy, he was older. He was in his mid forties. And so he wasn't as he used to be. He was slowing
down. He done did everything, and he was trying to go
home now. He had already did twenty-some years. I don't
even know for sure what he was in for. I believe a lot of
guys back then were robbing drug stores. They were
shooting dope. Getting morphine and Xanax and all that
stuff. I believe that's what he was in prison for.

Buddy taught me a lot. He taught me a *whole* lot. About
surviving. About dealing with people on their level and
staying mentally up on someone. About not being taken
advantage of. About protecting yourself without resorting
to violence. How to do it mentally. How to stay on top of
the situation. And, especially, not getting played.

He taught me about different people's personalities.
He was a good manipulator. He was real good at manipu-
lating people. He used the respect that they had for him
and the *like* that they had for him, to get things done for
himself. And he never did, that I know of, that I seen, mis-
use anybody. He used his strength for a lot of good. He
stopped a lot of trouble.

He once stopped a female officer from getting beat up.
He stopped inmates from tearing each other apart
because they respected him so much. He'd say, "Hey, man,
y'all come on. That don't mean no thing."

He done did do all that ignorant stuff in his childhood,
in his growing-up years, that he know'd what it was about.
When he talked, a person could listen and respect what he
was saying 'cause he'd been there. They knew this here

ain't no chump. He started riots. He shut whole blocks down himself. He took a liking to me and that's one of the reasons I didn't have no problems at Holman.

I was going to stab a man at Holman. I was *going* to. A man really disrespected me. I wasn't a homosexual back then. I didn't believe in it, didn't like it. This man was going to trump me with it, real ignorant like. Now, the whole mentality in prison is if somebody disrespects you like that, you have to deal with it.

Buddy seen what was going down. And everybody knew that Buddy really liked me and vice versa. We were buddies. I was going to my bed to get my knife, and Buddy grabbed the dude by his face and pushed him into the bars. Basically he took it up and did that 'cause something had to be done to the dude. He would rather do this than see me get a knife and take it to another level.

I believe Buddy actually had love for me. I was like his little brother. Oh, he was a big guy—oh, man. Buddy was probably the biggest white guy in the Alabama penal system. We're talking about a mountain of a man here. He's on the street now.

I got involved with leatherwork where they actually started a business, a leather shop. I learned how to carve and tool custom leather goods—saddles and boots and vests, wallets, belts, purses. And that's what I enjoy doing. I believe if I ever get out of prison that's what I would want to do. I realize I have to have a nine-to-five, actually a couple of them, when I first get out. Eventually, I'd like to use the Internet and go to different trade shows. I actually had a friend teach me that. He was also a guy who worked with me in the leather shop.

THE DEATH CHAMBER

We always knew when an electrocution went down. Oh, yeah. When I worked on the maintenance crew, I actually worked with the electrician. He was my boss. He was an electrician, and the day before an electrocution, he would do a test run, checking the generator.

You know all those stories about when the electric chair starts and the light dims? It's not true. [LAUGHING] No, it's not. The chair has its own separate power. I was not allowed to work on that, but I was present when it was tested. I seen how it was, how it was situated, the death cell, and all that. We were always working back there. But as far as putting my hands on it, no, I wasn't allowed to do that. In fact, that place and inside the cubes was the only area I was not allowed access to. The cubes are like the control center of the prison. That's a big security risk area.

I actually talked to one individual that was executed two days later. I can't remember the man's name. He was under observation. They was keeping an eye on him, I guess for suicide or whatever, I'm not sure. We were talking just like me and you. And I was asking him, you know, "Hey, man, how do you feel?" He wasn't that old. I'm guessing he was about twenty-five, twenty-six.

He was saying, "Man, I'd rather do this than spend the

rest of my life down the hall." I didn't believe him. I mean, who wants to die? But he was saying it with a straight face. I asked him if there was anything I could do for him. And if he asked me to do something, I'd have did it, no matter what it would be. If he wanted drugs, I would have gone down the hall and got 'em. I would have. But he didn't want anything. He said he was okay.

My boss man, the electrician, he was present, of course, when they took him into the room with the electric chair. He told me how he acted and what happened and this and that. He said that he finally broke down, right at the end. He was meeting death. The strongest human instinct is self-preservation, you know. For somebody to embrace death is not physically possible. You might be able to do it, but you are going against everything that's inside of you.

My boss man never talked about his feelings about putting a man to death. I actually asked him. And he said that he was just trying to do his job. He was trying not to deal with it, get involved. He didn't like it, I don't think.

Some of them do. The warden had no problem pulling the switch. None at all. I think if it had been up to him, he'd light the whole prison up. He was that type of hateful person. He didn't get along with nobody, and nobody liked him. He was just mean.

I ask myself, Do I believe in the death penalty? I've met some people in prison that I would never, ever want to be around any child, family member, friend, or anybody. They were literally amoral. They had no respect for life. Period. They had no morals, no values. None. Raping a child would

Easterling Correctional Facility

be nothing. Raping a dog would be nothing. I mean, they literally have no sense of right and wrong. What do you do with people like that? Do you put them in a cell for the rest of their life? Because you can't even put them in with the rest of the population 'cause they're so bad. Right now, in Holman, men are locked up alone for years, ten years or better, 'cause they can't be in the population. What do you do with them? Do you want to keep them in a cell? Or do you want to give them the death penalty?

If it was up to me, I would say keep them in a cell. I can't never say no man is ever above being redeemed. I believe that changes can take place in people. Spiritual changes that can change a person. Changes took place in me.

EASTERLING CORRECTIONAL FACILITY

Holman was a level-five prison, maximum security. This here is a level four, a medium-security facility. After level four, you go to honor camp, and then you have your work release. That was my intention, to come here and get a trade and go to an honor camp. An honor camp is a lower-level-security camp. It's the next stage before going to the street.

I wasn't here but three weeks when they changed the criteria. They said I was no longer eligible for any pre-release program. This is the lowest I can go—there is nothing better than this.

They changed the criteria because a man who had been in a work-release program killed a warden, the warden's wife, and some workers right in that area. I forgot how many people it was. And since the man was a violent offender, it was in the news. "Oh, they are letting violent offenders go to work release" and stuff like that. So they changed the criteria. I'm a violent offender. Heinous. Yes, that's what they call me.

I've been hearing *heinous* for so long now. I feel like these people don't know me. They don't know me! They always say the worst. The administration is always going to point out the worst about me. If you listen to them read

the case summary and progress review report, it's so negative and so mean, you can feel the venom behind it. It's
like they have a personal stake to make me look like an
animal. There's nothing positive in those reports. There's
no balance in it whatsoever. From the top to bottom, it's
negative.

I got to a point where I don't even care what they say.
They're still bringing up something I did when I was
twelve, fourteen years old. Here I'm twenty-six, I'm going
to be twenty-seven years old, and they're trying to hold
something against me from when I was fourteen. I know
they don't mean me no good. They don't want me to go
nowhere. After all, if it wasn't for me and people like me,
they wouldn't have no job.

It's hard when people who are supposed to be professional employees bring their personal prejudices and problems to work with them and take them out on you. I'm an
inmate, and they don't like me. They just don't like me. So
they mess me up, block me when I might be eligible for
something. They won't give it to me for the simple reason—I know it sounds petty—but they just don't like me.
They don't believe I should have it.

I actually lost hope. I gave up hope when they changed the
criteria for parole on me. They told me I can't go no further. This is it. I gave up. I said, "Okay, it's time to start living prison life. This is what it's going to be. A real horrible
life. Since I'm going to be in prison, probably for many,
many years, I'm going to try to make it as easy as I can."

Homosexual activity is real pervasive here. I've been

around homosexual activity for so long. After you're around it for so long, you become desensitized. It's no longer something crazy or weird, it becomes part of your environment.

I actually met an individual I have some strong feelings for. Being lonely, being in prison by myself all those years. It's a lonely life. Human beings are made to have some type of intimate contact with another individual. We use substitutes in prison. Sometimes a person might play the role of a woman. And you allow yourself to be tricked to thinking that this is the same thing as being with a female. You buy the story. You buy it because you're tired of being alone, because you're tired of that loneliness.

Right now, I call myself a bisexual. Well, I can't really say bisexual because I haven't been with a woman—a girl—for twelve years. I say "girl" 'cause I've never been with a woman in my life. When I was on the street, I had a couple girlfriends, whatever. I was a kid, you know. But that's it.

We have different classes for people in prison. You have people who may have certain types of homosexual dealings because they're afraid, or because they want somebody to give 'em stuff. Then you have individuals who been locked up for such a long time that they want it for companionship. A lot of times the sexual aspect is very rarely even involved. It's more for companionship and having somebody to care about. And to care about you. We try to make each other's time as easy as we can. That's what I'm doing. I'm just with one person.

Even in prison, you got diseases, you know what I'm saying? It's not as bad as on the street, but you got 'em. Me, myself, I feel like I would be disrespecting myself if I was to go running wild. Usually the people who are doing that don't respect themselves. It's like on the street, only with substitutes.

The other guys don't bother us. They don't have a choice. They know what would happen—they would be dealt with. You can't ask people in prison to leave you alone. You can't ask people in prison to respect you 'cause they don't respect that. You have to *make* them respect you. If they know that you'll do something to 'em, then they're going to leave you alone, unless they're just fools. Not too many are fools.

Sometimes I feel mean, especially toward certain individuals, bullies and people like that. I have a very bad reaction to them. Real bad. It's a whole 'nother side of me.

Since I've been in this prison, I hit a man in the face with a mop bucket for messing with me. He wouldn't leave me alone. I was minding my own business. He was trying to be a bully. I hit a lieutenant of the Southern Brotherhood with a mop, too. Now individuals know not to mess with this dude 'cause he's not going to let you get away with it. It's sad, but that's the way I have to be. Either that or they're going to run all over me. They'll push you around. They'll steal. They'll do all kinds of stuff to you. You can't ask for sympathy around here. It's a dog-eat-dog world.

You can do all the talking you want, but you have to use force, whether you want to or not. I'll kick a man in his face while he's asleep to make him leave me alone, to make him stop trying to touch me up, pushing on me, taking something from me. I figure just get it over with and deal with the consequences later. Then I don't have to worry about it.

My family went their own way for years. I haven't had a visit from my family in about five years. It's a long drive—they aren't financially able to make the trip. I might get a letter once every couple of months. My brother, who's in prison for the same time as me, has a different dad. His dad is a little more blessed, I think, more successful than mine. His dad's there for him. Me myself, my mom, my brothers, and my sister have gone our own way a long time ago. I don't know what happened. I mean, we never had a negative fall-out. I guess time did it. I'm used to doing time on my own.

I'd seen my mom when I was at the county jail. I never saw her when I was at Donaldson. My brothers and the sister-in-law I loved so much are divorced. I never saw her again. I remember when I was younger, like when I was in Donaldson, I used to see all the inmates get packages and stuff. Being still young, I had a lot of childish thoughts, like, Man, I wish I had a package. Little things like that used to bother me and used to make me angry and bitter toward my family. I felt like they should have been there for me.

My lawyer Bryan is the only one I have out there on the street. Bryan is the only person I call. He introduced me to a staff attorney who works in his office. Until today, you, they are the only people I talk to on the outside.

Bryan was the only person who's been there for me. I don't know why—he's just been there. If it weren't for him, I'd never receive any incentive packages or Christmas packages. He's the only person I have who does that. He just sent me money for some tennis shoes. I try to support myself the best I can. I do portraits and stuff like that.

This is my third prison, not counting the county jail. I've been here since '99. It's probably the most stressful one I've been to. It's really not designed for people that's got a lot of time to do. It's for people with shorter sentences. They are real, real strict. They write you up for just about anything, which messes up your parole record. Here you might be written up for having an extra plastic spoon, and they'll lock you up for it. For thirty days. Forty-five days. You may be written up for having an extra roll of toilet paper. It is written up as contraband. It usually doesn't say what kind of contraband. When the administration sees "contraband," they don't know if it's a knife, drugs, or what. So it's hard to keep a clean record here.

The dorms are real crowded. I'm in a dorm with about 130 beds that's only designed for about seventy-five or eighty, if I'm correct. We're all just packed in there together, head to foot. It's real crowded.

We sleep on steel bunks with a cotton mattress, just folded cotton and put in a plastic cover. I've pretty much gotten used to it. I probably couldn't sleep on a regular bed if I had one. We have boxes that go under the bed with a lock for our personal stuff. Windows? We have windows. But when you have that many people in such a small area, it's real stuffy. We have ventilation fans, but they're not doing much good. In summertime, it will get up to ninety plus degrees on the inside. It's really hot.

There's nothing to do, there's nothing productive to do. You got grown men lying in bed all day watching soap operas. That's not healthy. They have trade schools, and they have GED school. I already have my GED. I got that when I was in Holman.

I'm actually trying to transfer away from this prison to another facility that would be a little better for me. So I don't want to get involved right now in a trade school and then transfer in a couple months. I think I'm going to wait that out and transfer and take my trade school in another facility. I would like to have a welding or automotive program. They may have a carpentry trade.

We have assigned jobs but not for money. It may be a kitchen worker or something like that. Myself, right now, I'm unassigned. I don't have a job right now. I spend my time with my artwork, with my music. I play electric guitar. It's not a personal guitar—we have one in the gym. Me and another man, we play together. I like sixties and seventies music, anything from folk, soul, blues, rock and roll. I'm not real crazy about jazz, though. It's a hard form of music to play. I don't like it, don't want to learn to play it. I've got a few associates that I talk with. I'm just waiting for the football season to start. That's how I spend my time.

Fights are usually gang related or about homosexual stuff. Homosexuals are pretty much accepted here. A lot of officers say that it keeps down trouble 'cause most of them that participate become informants and stuff of that nature.

The main racketeering that's going on here are people

Mark's portrait of a prisoner in his bunk

that have their own hustles, just like the street. You have
people who are good at maybe running tattoos, running
stores, loan stuff out for money and interest.

Then you have the artists. Myself, I'm a portrait artist. I
do inmates' portraits. I don't do it for free 'cause it's a lot
of work. In fact, I just got through spending a year in
lockup because of an unpaid fee. I had done two portraits

for a man, and I didn't charge him but seventeen dollars. They were black-and-white sketches, whereas most of the time I work in pastels. And the man didn't pay me. He owed me for two months. Well, when I went to confront the man about the money he owed me—I didn't go with any thought of violence or nothing like that—I said, "You know, I need my money."

The man had a crutch, like the one I have now. (I just slipped coming out of the shower.) He tried to hit me with it in front of everybody. Anyway, I hit him and ended up doing an extra year for it. And that's what I'm trying to stay away from. I didn't really mean it for real. But when somebody jumps at you, that's how it is. I was in lockup for thirteen months plus a month in the hospital. So that's fourteen months altogether.

Lockup is *hot*! Hot and boring. You ain't got nothing in there at all. It's hard to get any reading materials. You can, but it's hard. They don't allow a library back there or anything. The only library is a law library, so it's real hard to get any type of reading material back there. You can't get anything sent in, no newspapers or books. You can catch the store for fifteen dollars a week, unless you are in the disciplinary stage. But convicts find ways to get anything. If anything is down there, I'll find a way to get it.

I think there's nothing I haven't been through. And what I mean by that is in prison there's nothing I haven't did. I've been involved in everything from homosexual activities to gambling, to fighting, to just anything you could think of. The worst of the worst that you can think of, I've been involved in. Before and in prison. Period.

I had never been involved in homosexual activity till I come to this place here. I partook in everything there is to partake of, trying to find out who I was, and what I wanted to be. Who was I? A majority of the time, I didn't know what I wanted until after I run into a wall. I may try something and realize that's not me.

I've got a lot of bitterness inside me. Yes, I do. I'm a miserable person, for real. Yesterday I was actually telling an individual who I'm pretty close with that sometimes I feel better about other people than I do about myself. I'm not able to make myself happy. I'm not able to find peace with myself. I do believe that I cursed myself and threw myself away. I believe that I will always suffer for what I did till the day I die. I know that. There's no doubt in my mind.

Even if I could be forgiven, I still can't escape the consequences. I still can't escape the law. I still can't escape the condition that put me here. There's no way around that. Sometimes I can forgive myself somewhat for what I did because I don't see myself as the same individual I was back then. In reality, I am that person, but my mind is different. I would never, ever, under any circumstances do that. That's the one thing that helps me, allows me, to forgive myself a little. Sometimes I feel like I'm serving a sentence for something that somebody else did.

I deserve to be punished, no doubt about it. But, after you've been in prison for so long, it ceases to be a punishment. It becomes just a way of life. The first few years, learning to adjust to prison is the punishment. Once you've adjusted, it isn't punishment anymore.

So where's the punishment then? You not doing nothing but institutionalizing a person. You know when the punishment is going to come back? When you get out of prison, have to adjust to the street. That's going to be another punishment. I believe I can do it. I believe I can do it through work. I'm going to have to keep myself very busy. I'm going to have to stay somewhere in touch with the environment that I left, at least for a while. Maybe I can even work around other inmates, or troubled kids, or somebody who's got something to do with prison life. Because that's what I know. It's scary out there, but, yeah, I believe I can do it.

I talked with Bryan yesterday. I said, "You know, I realize what you're always telling me, the hard thing is not getting out of prison, it's staying out." It took me several years to get adjusted to prison life, and it will take some years to get adjusted to the street. Being locked up in prison, the things we take real, real serious, may not be serious to the same degree. It's a whole different value system.

I'd like to go back on the street. I'd like to help change just one person's life. One. I want to help somebody that doesn't have anybody, and I want it to be a somebody that's really messed up. I don't want an easy case because I wasn't an easy case. Other than that, I can't say what I do because I don't know.

■ ■ ■

There's something about taking an individual's life that kills a part of you. It's a slow death. I'll suffer till the day I die, there's no doubt about it. I'll never have children. Never. For the simple reason I believe in a generational curse. I believe in things of that nature. Man, I look around and I tell myself there are enough children alive today that don't have anybody. Why put another one in the world where there's enough here already?

I don't have any contact with the family of the man I killed. It's hard to understand, I know, but I do not feel like the same individual that did that. I really don't. That wasn't me. I know it's strange. What have I got? Another personality? No. Who I am today is not the same person who did that. The Mark then was a fourteen-year-old *fool*, trying to be grown up, not knowing how. Didn't care about anybody. Didn't care about himself.

I ask myself, What's to be done with my life now? I still don't have the answers. I don't know if they're going to let me out of prison. Ever. I ask myself a lot of questions: What can I do now that I've done this? What kind of faith can I have? What kind of life can I lead with this in my past? It's never going to leave me. It never will. A theft or a burglary can leave you, but a murder can't.

I done wear your batteries down.

CHAPTER THREE

Look at Me

In March 2005, when five of the nine Supreme Court justices agreed that no offender under the age of eighteen was eligible for the death penalty, seventy-one men were supposed to be immediately removed from the nation's death rows.

Four months after this decision, I traveled to Texas to meet a young man who was seventeen when he was sent to death row. He was still there.

On the night of May 13, 1992, a Californian, Nanon Williams, seventeen, and some of his older acquaintances, Vaal G., Patrick S., and Elaine W., went to a secluded park in Houston, Texas, to carry out a cocaine deal with Adonius Collier and Emmade Rasul.

The state alleged that Adonius and Emmade were unarmed but that Nanon had a shotgun and a .25 derringer magnum, and Vaal carried a .22 pistol.

Shots were fired. One bullet hit Emmade in the face, and a second one hit his foot. Miraculously, he got away. Adonius was not so lucky. He was shot twice in the head, first by the pistol and then by the shotgun. He died.

Some of Nanon's tattoos, photographed through the Plexiglas of the visiting area

The police recovered only one of the weapons involved in the crime, Vaal's .22. Twenty-one-year-old Vaal immediately hired a lawyer and, sometime later, turned himself in to the police. During an audiotaped statement, Vaal admitted that he fired his .22 at Adonius Collier. He pleaded guilty to a reduced charge—illegal investment in drugs—in exchange for his testimony against Nanon.

The following August, Nanon was arrested at his home in Los Angeles and was extradited to Texas.

Throughout the trial, the prosecutor argued that Nanon killed Collier with his .25 handgun and the shotgun. Vaal testified against Nanon, claiming that he never even shot in the direction of Collier. Under questioning by the defense, Vaal admitted that he had given a contradictory statement to the police. Robert Baldwin, the Houston Police Department's ballistics expert, also testified. He told the jury that there was no doubt, no doubt at all, that a bullet found in Adonius Collier's head was from Nanon's .25-caliber gun. He said that it was impossible that the bullet could have come from Vaal's .22. In fact, he was so certain he did not even bother to test fire Vaal's gun.

Based on the testimony of the codefendant eyewitness, who had made a deal to escape the death sentence, and the ballistics findings, the jury voted to convict Nanon Williams for capital murder.

The information in this chapter is from the many letters we wrote to each other and from my interview with Nanon on death row. For the interview, the prison's press director allowed us two hours rather than the usual forty-five minutes. While we were talking, though, we didn't know how much time we'd have. To save time, Nanon would often reply, "That's in the book. . . . You can get that in the book." With his permission, I've included excerpts from his book Still Surviving *to fill in the text. These excerpts (which start on page 92), plus additional information from his lawyers, are indented.*

May 7, 2005
Dear Susan:

I received your letter today. Today is Friday, but mail

doesn't go out until Monday. Before I go on, I have a manual typewriter that is prehistoric and on the verge of becoming extinct. The keys lock and more. . . . Besides, I just type bad. Please overlook the mistakes. I am sitting here drinking coffee like it's old cheap whiskey and I hit the wrong keys like a reckless drunk. Bear with me. (Smile)

All journalists are brought to the actual visitation area at 1:00 P.M. We are supposed to be brought out an hour in advance, at 12:00 P.M., so you not only will not see the handcuffs being taken off, but everything is set up in advance: what booth, where they want us, etc. . . . Come prepared to get straight to work. And, yes, you can take as many pictures as you wish. You can bring a *[video]* recorder if you wish, but keep in mind that we have to talk through phones. Your side has two phones. You can use one to tape a microphone on while we talk on the other. I don't know what you know or don't know. Just thought I would mention it in advance.

In struggle,
Nanon

May 10, 2005

Dear Susan:

Enclosed you will find all kinds of stuff, including pictures. Please return everything, as those are the copies I keep in my cell. Read my other book, *The Darkest Hour*. To learn more about my life, read the chapter "When God Wakes Up." The book can be ordered at Amazon, or ask my mom to send it to you.

I DID sign the paperwork to see you so don't let them tell you otherwise.

In struggle,
Nanon

May 19, 2005

Dear Susan:

I'm sure there are many things to cover about prison. I wrote all these books by the age of twenty-five. I'll be thirty-one in a few months. I see things differently. I can not only cover "what" happens, but the "why"s. Anyway, let's just get together and start yakking! (Smile)

Dealing with prison, man, there is much not covered. Even in dealing with crimes, I can compare those who did crimes either through desire or anger. In your mind, what is the worst—one done in anger or desire? And why? Unconsciously, prisoners associate with others who they have compatibility with but they don't know why.

Here it is quite easy to separate sexual predators from others. We'll talk about that. Bring a recorder.

I was moved to a "management cell." There are two cells like this in the entire prison. I occupy one now. Why? Haven't violated any rules. . . . It's dark. Can't see anything. There is no power in my cell. Can't hear anything hardly. I'm using the light at the bottom of my door to write. I hope I haven't made too many mistakes.

I look forward to seeing you.

In struggle,
Nanon

DEATH ROW,

LIVINGSTON, TEXAS

Wednesday is media day at the Texas Department of Criminal Justice (TDCJ). The prison, off a quiet country road, appears, like Oz, from nowhere. Except for the layers and layers and layers of razor wire, the low, flat, beige stone building looks like a well-run factory. The lawn is green and perfectly cut. Flowers line the walkways. There are no dead flowers, not one brown-edged petal, not one yellow leaf. The parking lot is huge, filled with pickups and SUVs. Bumper stickers sport yellow ribbons, American flags, and SUPPORT OUR TROOPS *decals.*

The director of public relations had called earlier with instructions: no open-toed shoes, sleeveless shirts, or shorts. Personal items

Allan B. Polunsky Unit

and money stay in the car. Bring lipstick inside, though, or it'll melt in the heat—the PR director is a woman.

Wallet and cell phone go into the glove compartment. A driver's license, tape recorder, and two cameras come into the prison.

Inside the visitors' entrance, a female officer sits behind a thick Plexiglas partition. It looks like the cockpit of a 747. She takes my driver's license and asks the prisoner's number: 999163. Another guard, a big, beefy guy, looks through the camera bag. Everyone's smiling, joking, friendly.

In Alabama, when I talked to Roy and Mark, there had been long, private contact visits. Here in Texas, thick, bulletproof Plexiglas separates inmate from interviewer. There is no physical contact at all.

The PR woman arrives to escort me to the visitors' area. She's pretty. Friendly. Chatty.

Creak! The first remote-controlled steel gate opens. Whooosh! *The second gate opens. "Welcome to the Roach Motel." A guard laughs. "Once you go in, you don't come out."*

The visitors' lounge smells institutional clean, like a school cafeteria. On one side of the room, there is a row of vending machines. On the other side, there's a long series of workstation-like cubicles. Each numbered cubicle faces a Plexiglas enclosure. On either side hang the two phones that Nanon described. The Plexiglas reflects the glare of the vending machines. Taking photographs will be hard. Impossible! The light is ugly, and the glare is awful.

Beyond the glare sits Nanon. He's locked inside a cube of steel and wire mesh. I feel like I know him.

The PR woman attaches a gadget between the recorder and the phone. "This will make it easier to tape." She smiles. It will also make it easier for the officers to listen in.

My right and his left hand touch the separating Plexiglas.

NANON: Look at my tattoos. I got tattoos all over my back. I got tattoos all over my chest. What you see is a shield of armor. This is not Nanon Williams. This is the kid in me using my body as a platform to say I'm tough. Hey, back off. Here's my shield of protection. I put a frown on my face.

Look at my picture. That's me as a kid. Look at my eyes. I was lost. What you see was me not searching for who I was.

I was judged a monster before I even knew who I was.

Every attempt is made to make me what I never was. My body and my size—I used to be way bigger than I am now—says I'm tough, now leave me alone. Instead of making me less fearful than I was, I became the image that you see. I wouldn't back down from anything. I didn't even realize that I became lost. It was fear.

Few men survive here. Years ago, perhaps they did. Not anymore. The visitation area looks nice. When you enter this prison, it resembles a college campus. Never allow appearances to fool you—you are entering a killing camp. Back where I am, there is metal upon metal, concrete, and cage after cage lined up with less than the space animals are afforded at the zoo. They will never, not ever, allow you to see and hear the madness around me back in the cells.

I have seen over 250 men executed. Men I knew. While most kids went to bars, clubs, school, I lived in a war zone. I have seen men raped, beaten to death, found hung in their cells, burned, cut. I have heard men scream so loud it feels like their voice is in your head. Death row is no place for a kid.

We prisoners all wear the same color, white, with DR printed in black on our backs. We must all be clean-shaven and have the same length hair. The aim is to strip away your identity, first through distinguishable physical characteristics. If all the prisoners look alike, the hope is that they act alike. They become programmed. If you were here, the goal would be to no longer allow Susan Kuklin to be Susan Kuklin. You would have a number.

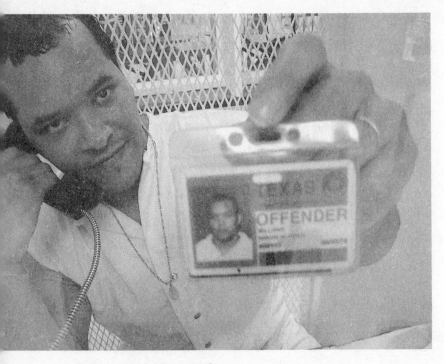

Nanon with ID card

My number is 999163. That's not my identification number; that's my death number. This number is based on the order in which you come to death row. A lot of times, they try to kill you in that order. It's your death number, right? They make me recite it all day. You gotta put it on your mail. You gotta say it every time they come to count you. You gotta say it to get trays—999163. It replaces me being Nanon. They ask for the number half the time before they ask you your name. In order to come to visit you, I had to say "Nanon Williams, 999163."

Every time I leave the cell, I gotta get handcuffed, even just to go to the shower. The skin on my hands is raw from being handcuffed so much. Look. My ankles, too. Sometimes they put a hockey mask over my face. It prevents me from biting them. I ain't never bit nobody. In fact, I haven't caught a serious disciplinary case in seven years. They put a mask on my face today. I said, "Now why you putting a mask on my face?"

"Well, you going to a legal visit or not?"

They want me to say no, and then you come up here and you be pissed off that you don't get to see me. Nine times out of ten, they would rather get you to believe that I refused to see you instead of explaining the reason why I'm not here. The mask was my compromise with myself today. The reason why I did it now is, if I come here and talk to you, I could reach a lot of people. If they want me to put on a mask, I could deal with it. Whereas before I wouldn't let them do that.

There are certain things I refuse to do regardless of the consequence. It's my way of letting myself know I'm still alive, that I'm still worth something to fight for. We always know what we're fighting against, but we don't know what we're fighting for. I'm fighting to keep a part of me, who I was before I came to prison. I wasn't a bad dude. I did stupid things as a kid, but I wasn't a bad dude. A lot of guys, when they come to prison, they give up on what they believe in. They surrender a little bit of themselves. They betray themselves, and they don't know why.

Now, I still won't bend down. I ain't bending down for

nothing. I ain't bending down and spreading my ass cheeks and all that stuff. I ain't doing that. But I learned to pick and choose what's worth it and what's not worth it.

See these sideburns here? We're not supposed to have them. It's against prison rules here in Texas. This is a rule violation. That's my way of being defiant. It's me being slick. I know what I can get away with and what I cannot get away with, and that is just the truth. For so many years, I refused to shave. Instead of compromising me, they said, "Well, if he ain't bothering nobody, we might as well leave him alone."

When I was arrested for capital murder, I was put with people who were coming *[to the county jail]* on appeal from death row. I listened to their stories about the guys who were on death row, but I really didn't pay any mind. I believed in justice, so to speak. I never believed it would be me.

> My attorney believed me to be innocent of the alleged crime but asked me to seriously consider taking a life sentence, instead of risking a trial and being condemned to death. Needless to say, I did not take it. Did I consider it? HELL NO!!! I am no choirboy, and yes, I am guilty of many things, but not of killing anyone.

In my case, I'm here because I was the only one who refused to give a statement to the police. Another guy even confessed on tape. I refused to take a deal. I was taught not to talk to the police. I was raised *never* to talk to the police: "You got a statement?" "No! Call my mamma!"

In Los Angeles, when we saw the police, we ran. I watched them beat us, not be cool to us. Never tell the police nothing! In my sick, twisted code of gangsterism, a code of silence, which to me was a form of honor, I will suffer for the rest of my life.

My attorney was appointed by the court. I felt that since she was paid by the state, she would try to satisfy the one who's paying the paycheck. So I didn't talk to her. But she wasn't like that at all. She worked on my case just like any other paid attorney. Later, she found out that the prosecutor gave false ballistics testimony. She was, like, "You didn't do this—why you never say nothing?" I didn't know what ballistics was.

SENTENCING

When the judge slowly repeated that I was to die, he smiled with a smirk. My mother, man, she was crying and shaking her head. She was almost hysterical. My sister was crying. Seeing their pain, I fell into my seat. I just sat there while everyone else was standing. I don't remember what happened after that. I remember being in a holding tank. The sheriffs in Harris County jail were told to take me to my cell, and I wouldn't move. When they forcefully moved me, I fought.

Later, when my mom came to see me, she sat there crying

and rocking herself. I did the same. My mother always knew I didn't do this. She told me God will make everything okay. At the time, it went in one ear and out the other.

NANON BECOMES NANON

LETTER FROM NANON: When you write about my childhood, the one thing I ask of you is please understand, do not allow my life to further cast a negative shadow over my family. Enough has been done. My childhood, it can read like a horror story, yet in many cases it is not. I do not want my childhood to be told without a great deal of understanding. I don't want to come across as someone who never had a chance. I did. I had a mother who gave me the very best in life. She always had the best intentions and made sure we had what we needed.

My mother became a registered nurse with a host of other degrees. My older sister graduated college with honors and is an accountant. My younger sister is a dietician, and my little brother, who is now twenty-two years old, just graduated from Notre Dame with a degree in journalism. But that's their story to tell without my life casting a cloud over them.

I need to tell you what events led to me thinking this way, not knowing better. You need to know the whys. But I want the focus on me, not them.

Nanon as a child (opposite)

■ ■ ■

I was born in Los Angeles, California. I grew up seeing people in the fast lane, hanging in Watts with my father, stepfather, and uncle. My father was one of the ghetto superstars, the person who ran everything, the shot caller. That's what my father was. In some cases, that's what my mother was. They were strong. They were smart.

Growing up, I admired the somebody who was a *somebody* in the ghetto. Somebody who was tough. I watched as people struggled and hustled to reach for the American dream, a dream that seemed to always pass them by. In the ghetto we taught each other responsibility through the trades and the hustles we learned from the streets. Where I grew up, in Watts, I didn't wake up idolizing the schoolteacher that learned us, I grew up watching the pimp, the prostitute, the hustler on the block. I didn't see them as bad people. I saw them trying to take care of their families, even though they didn't realize they were like a collection of wolves fighting for the one little chicken.

As for school, I guess you could say I have little formal education. I never graduated from high school. From kindergarten to third grade, I went to a private Catholic school called St. Frances Cabrini. Those were the happiest years of my life.

When I was five years old, I got stabbed in my leg for my bike. I was five years old! I watched my mother fight off intruders when our house was invaded. My uncle was shot and killed. My earliest memory is my hands covering his throat to stop the blood flow. I was so covered in blood, paramedics thought I was shot.

After a series of shootings, our house getting robbed, an attempted assassination on my father, everyone felt it was best for me to live with my grandparents in Dickinson, Texas. I lived in too many places to keep up with. LA, Dickinson, Cincinnati, Tennessee, Alabama, and back to LA. At one point, I moved to my mother and stepfather's ranch in Ahwahnee, California. They owned this ninety-nine-acre ranch where they bred Arabian horses, and my stepfather had a drug lab. I guess you could say all my life I knew about drugs, even how to make them. My step-father treated me like I was his blood son. He loved me and still does.

The ranch was high in the mountains near Yosemite. It was a white area where they never saw a person of color. They called me "red nigger." I didn't know what red nigger was. Kids wouldn't play with me. Later, one guy told me they thought I was an outcast. My teacher told my mother I was dyslexic. They put me in a trailer, away from the other kids. No one talked to me. I was held back in fourth grade. I felt stupid.

I figured they didn't want me in the class, so I quit going to school. I didn't go to hardly any of my fourth-grade year. My mother didn't know about it. No one knew. I stayed in the woods all day. No one ever bothered to inform my parents that I didn't go to school. That year, my father was gunned down over a drug territory dispute.

From fifth to eighth grade—half of eighth—I went to school in Dickinson, Texas. I made excellent grades, was on honor roll, made junior Olympics in track, was on the All-State soccer team, All-Star Little League Baseball, and made first team on football. I did well.

My mother returned to Los Angeles and wanted me back, so I went back. The second half of my eighth-grade year was spent at a gang-infested school where basically all the outcasts were sent. That was my neighborhood's district school. In my ninth-grade year, I returned to Dickinson, in Texas. My tenth-grade year was back to Los Angeles, but this time I went to a private Catholic school called Junipero Serra. I was on the varsity team and received national recognition for football. I was in the newspapers every week, in college scouting magazines for upcoming recruits. I also started accepting money and gift certificates from football scouts. By the end of my tenth year, my mother was unable to afford the school's tuition. I was sent to Leuzinger High School. At the time, it was considered one of the most violent schools in America. Riots often erupted between the black students and the Hispanics. We were searched and had to go through metal detectors upon entering school.

The school was gang infested. I fought a lot there. I was looked upon as the preppie kid from the private school. I also boxed and even had sponsors. I guess you could say I excelled at boxing more than anything because I fought a

Nanon in football uniform (opposite)

lot at Leuzinger. My reputation got me suspended for the constant fighting. I started hanging with a different crowd. I started ditching school.

Like I said earlier, while my mother was raising me and my siblings, she went to school to become a registered nurse. But we were on welfare. I watched my mother working so hard. I watched her struggling. I knew I had to do something to help. I was the eldest male child. I wanted to be the man of the house. I started selling drugs. First marijuana, then crack. I became tied up in the streets. I wanted to make things easier somehow, but I did more harm than good. I should have stayed focused on sports and getting my scholarship and school. I was a fool.

During the day, after school, after the football season was over, I boxed at Hoover Gym. At night I sold drugs. My mom didn't know. But the fridge was filled with food. New TVs popped up at the house. I got my siblings stuff. And I felt good because I was helping. I didn't think about what drugs did to people. My reward was the smiles from those I loved. They did not know what I was doing. Eventually, this led me to a camp in a juvenile facility.

I was sentenced to nine months at a juvenile facility called Camp Kilpatrick, in Malibu. Camp Kilpatrick was a juvenile facility, but it was also a sports camp designed to teach kids teamwork and how to sacrifice for others. We had a football team called the Camp Kilpatrick Mustangs. We played extremely rich private schools. We were good. Truth is, our team had some of the baddest kids in the system. Gangbangers with tattoos, violent crimes. And we pummeled the rich kids. I guess you could say I loved the camp, although it was jail. Why? I excelled. I was the team leader. I even got awards as "the best all-around scholar." I received honors in football. If you read my trial transcripts, you will see that my counselor, Howard Gold, testified on my behalf.

Upon release, I was sent back to Leuzinger, where I was quickly accused of getting in trouble. It wasn't true. I was trying to do well. Scouts were watching me and anticipating my senior season. What happened was a car had been stolen. The police went looking for me at school. I didn't want to go back to the camp so I ditched school, and that violated my probation. They later found out I didn't steal the car, but by running and ditching school, I was in trouble.

By sixteen, I quit caring. I ended up visiting my grandparents in Texas. Three months later, I was arrested for capital murder. I was seventeen years old. I have never seen the light of day since.

TO DEATH ROW

Sometime after the conviction, when the guards came to get me, I was stripped down to my boxer shorts and staring with a faraway look in my eyes that unnerved the gathering deputies. When they were ready to transfer me to prison, I refused to comply. I refused to comply with everything. So even before arriving on death row, I had been hit with a Taser gun. It's a stun gun, but there are different kinds. Some have electric-like balls that shoot out, some with wires, some with electricity. I still have a permanent bruise on my leg and back.

"Bend over and spread 'em!" a lieutenant called from behind the mechanical doors that open the cells into the corridor. He spoke with a Texas redneck drawl, a sound that will always be a nightmare to me.

"Do what?"

"Bend over and spread your ass cheeks and cough, inmate!"

"I'm not bending over to spread shit, so do what you gotta do!" Those bastards! I thought. Who in hell did they think I was? Did they really believe I was going to bend over and spread my ass cheeks for them?

In war they strip captured prisoners naked. They know the naked prisoner will be embarrassed about their sexuality. The guards don't understand what they're doing, but the people who implement these rules clearly understand what they're doing. If they told you right now, "Hey, strip naked," you'd be so focused on your own sexuality that they could slap you around and you'd still be focused on covering up your privates. When they make us bend over and spread our butts, or lift our feet, our tongue, we're embarrassed. We become submissive to a point where we will do anything they tell you because you want to hurry up and get your clothes on. I fought it.

The corridor opened. Metal helmets. Steel batons. Taser guns. Padded vests. Like an army platoon. "Inmate! Bend over and spread your ass cheeks, or physical force will be applied."

"I ain't bending over and spreading my ass like an animal for your pleasure."

Before I could finish the words, the Taser gun was fired and hit my left thigh, sending a shockwave through my body that made me extremely dizzy. My vision blurred. I smelled the burned flesh of my thigh, and I braced myself against the concrete wall for support as I slid to the floor.

I attempted to rise to my feet again, but I was hit again in the chest with the Taser gun. The metal ball that shot out this time didn't seem to affect me at all, so I lunged toward the lieutenant with all my might, knocking him to the floor as my fist crashed against his chin. Before I could strike him again, the other deputies wrestled me to the floor, and all of them piled on top of me. I was handcuffed and shackled, lying on my stomach, the lieutenant began choking me, repeatedly screaming, "You dumb son of a bitch! This is how it will feel before they kill you!" He continued to yell as I drifted in and out of consciousness.

WELCOME TO DEATH ROW—ELLIS ONE UNIT

I arrived in the van staring at the prison called Ellis One Unit *[in Huntsville, Texas]*. We arrived at the back gate. I saw a tower, a gunman, an electric gate wrapped with barbed wire. Before the guards took me out, I was shackled and masked. I was angry, and I showed it. They were scared of me, ready to pounce on me at any moment.

"Remember who you are, not what they make you out to be," I said to myself. We went down a long hallway. I met the death row captain, who

Ellis One Unit

sat behind the desk in his leather chair looking as if he thought he was the god of some lost island. I chuckled to myself as I stared at him, That damn fool!

"Williams, how old are you, boy?"

"I'm not your boy!"

"Well, let me put it this way. What is your god-damn age, you smart-ass?"

Prisoners called the deputies Boss Man, a slave term. From day one, I called the guards Officer. Sometimes I called them Pig.

The sergeant told me I was going to G-15, Cell 13, on 1 Row. "These wings aren't that bad and will allow you to be around prisoners who are less violent or simply don't want trouble. If you give us problems, I'll personally send you to a wing called J-21, and believe me," he said with a threatening tone, "no one wants to go there."

Months went by.

I was in recreation doing my exercises and playing a little basketball with my friend Tex. It was a nice, sunny day, and I was feeling good. A guard approached. "Williams, time to rack up!"

Needless to say, I wasn't going to do that, not ever, not under any circumstances! A decent day quickly turned terrible as the guard entered the day room acting big and bad to impress the female guard who stood behind the door.

"I said, bend over and spread 'em!" He placed his hand on my shoulder.

"Punk! You don't put your hands on me!" I slung his hand away. "Bitch! Who do you think I am for you to touch on me?" I walked toward him and he began backpedaling away from me.

A few minutes later, a new sergeant appeared, one that I never saw before. He told me he was going to handcuff me and take me down to the office to talk to me. I followed his instructions, not thinking that things would get any worse. When we got closer to the office, we suddenly stopped. The steel door we stopped in front of had a wooden plate that read J-21.

"What's this?" I asked.

"This is J-21, inmate. This will be your new home for a while."

J-21

There was black steel-mesh wire covering the bars, enclosing the cells so tightly that no object could be pushed in or out. The tiers seemed very, very dark because no light could penetrate the windows, yet you could still tell the difference between day and night. There was so much steel, wire, and other junk blocking off the view that even the air seemed thin as I took a deep breath

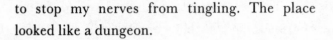

to stop my nerves from tingling. The place
looked like a dungeon.

When I entered the cellblock, it was loud. As I walked past
the cells, there were shouts—guys were sizing me up. I was
scared, Susan. I was over 230 pounds, my arms were
twenty-one inches wide, muscles everywhere from driving
myself to get bigger and stronger. With a bald head and a
scowl on my face, I imagine guys knew I was not to be
messed with. Inside, I was scared, very scared. I knew that
this was no place for a boy.

Cell thirteen.

I'll never forget just how little that cell looked as
the doors opened and those steel bars slammed
shut behind me. The cell was nine feet by ten
feet. Everything looked old and rusty and
crusted with dirt. In one corner ants were crawl-
ing in and out of a hole in the ceiling. A huge,
pregnant cockroach ran for cover behind a metal
box that was supposed to be a shelf for my property. Hanging from the wall with steel hooks was
a steel slab that was supposed to be a bed. When
I sat down I felt cold run up and down my spine.
Behind me a yellow lightbulb glowed and seemed
to produce the only heat in the cell.

Look at me. I'm black, but I'm also mixed with Indian
and French. In prison people look distinctly Hispanic,
distinctly black. I don't look distinctly anything. So who did I

link up with? I was a loner. I didn't have anyone. Eventually, I made friends, but for the wrong reasons. The wrong reasons were people looked up to me 'cause I fought the guards. When I first got to death row, I would not talk to a guard for nothing. They didn't exist to me. If they hit me, I hit them back. Guards or prisoners, I didn't see the difference if a guard assaulted me or if a prisoner assaulted me. I hit back.

On my first day in recreation, I had already made up my mind that the first advance, or threat, or smart remark, I would pounce the guy. It didn't happen. I actually met my first friends—Jazz (John Barefield), Big Tex (Vincent Cook), Stumpa (Dominique Green), Rogers-El (Patrick Rogers), Da'Oud (Dwight Adanandus), and Slim (James Aldridge). They are all dead now.

Stumpa was in the next cell. He got me some soap and a towel so I could scrub down my cell. He gave me my new name. A lot of guys make up names. You know, "psycho" this and that. It's their way of keeping a part of them within themselves. So in turn, that's a shield. See this tattoo here? LA. That's what people called me. That was the nickname given to me by the prisoners because I was the only one not from Texas. Little by little, Nanon was no more. I became LA. Now I tell people to call me by my name. I want to be the man my mamma named.

Look at it this way—it's an analogy that a psychologist posed to me. If you take a pup from his mother too soon, two things can happen to that pup: He either learns how to adapt and survives, or he perishes. I adapted.

I wake up every day with five hundred convicted killers,

not to say who's innocent or guilty. I wake up every day knowing that some people will try to hurt me. They believe you are a monster. You are a killer. Whether or not it's true, you are convicted of murder, so violence escalates to the extreme.

The guys were all older than me, so everyone was trying to tell me what not to do and what to do. The first persons I was really, really close to was Jazz and Rogers-El. They were the type of men who would reach out and try to educate people. Most times I could tell what was happening, but I couldn't explain *why* it was happening. They would try to teach me the whys. I was a kid, a fool. A fool doesn't know he's a fool until it's pointed out.

> Here I was in the worst place prison had to offer, death row, and the worst wing that the prison claimed they had on death row. To be truthful, I had the feeling that the many months in prison changed me and made me so numb inside that perhaps my own sanity was slipping away.

As a kid dealing with this, I wondered, How can things get worse? Dealing with execution. Looking at guys going crazy. Looking at guys spreading shit on their faces. Looking at guys getting killed. Looking at guards beating you.

I was the youngest guy on J-21. Being young helped me, I believe, instead of hurt me. The next oldest person was to become my best friend, Emerson Rudd. We called him Young Lion. I'm saving to get him a headstone now. I have pictures of his funeral. Young Lion was a couple of years older than me. Before the laws changed, you had guys on death row twenty, fifteen, twenty-five years. Now everybody is executed quick under the antiterrorist death penalty laws, so you don't have the collection of older prisoners. When I say older, I don't mean age, I mean the experiences that could strategically teach others how to do something constructive, like teach each other how to read and write. We don't have that here now. But back then, the older guys were trying to be big brothers to me. I learned from them, even though in my mind everyone here was a hick. [SMILES]

The sad part is, when smart prisoners understand how they torture people psychologically, they use it against the rest of us. They themselves become manipulative.

There are people here *[on J-21]* who will see how far they can go with you. From day one, I was always quick to fight, so when I first got here, I kicked, fought, whatever. One time when I got into a fight, I lost myself. One time a dude disrespected me. He was bigger than me, 280 pounds, way bigger than me. Even though he started it, and he was wrong in my mind, I kept hitting him and hitting him when I should have stopped. I forgot what I was doing. I didn't even recognize that I was still fighting. They sent him to the hospital. They sent me to solitary. I was twenty-one at the time.

Most of the time I was at Ellis, I lived in solitary. At the time, you could only stay in solitary a maximum of fifteen days at a time. My time was stacked. What they would do with me and Emerson is take us to solitary for fifteen days, then bring us back to J-21 for one day, then back to solitary. Whenever I was brought back to J-21, I was placed in a "management cell." Sometimes I would stay on J-21 up to a week and then get taken back to solitary. With the exception of three months, I was in solitary the whole time I was in Ellis Unit, basically for years. So in the minds of the other prisoners, it was, like, *that dude is crazy*.

The sad part is I had developed a disregard for my own life. Because I'd been through so much, I didn't care. I just didn't care no more. I developed a disregard for my life to a point where I was suicidal, yet too much a coward to end my life. I was suicidal in standing up to the wrongs the guards did to me, or to the other prisoners. We were beaten, thrown in solitary, starved, kicked like a stray dog while handcuffed. When you feel too much pain, you seek refuge. Some find it through jumping into the abyss of insanity. Some cut on themselves to see if they are alive. I found refuge in anger.

One time, I woke up in solitary butt naked, handcuffed, and shackled in my cell. I'd been gassed. Ten guards ran in on me and pepper sprayed me for hours. I didn't care. I just didn't care. I didn't care if I died. I didn't care if I was executed. I just didn't care. I understood that people have a breaking point, and my breaking point was I had quit believing in anything. I wasn't crazy, but in some ways, I lost myself.

A SOLITARY LIFE

Solitary helped me. Living in solitary, you have nothing to do but look in the mirror. It made me think about

everything I've been through in my life, everything my
mother taught me. That's when I began reading and
writing. The more I read, the more I realized how little I
knew. Books are like a mirror into your own life. They help
you relate and understand your own experiences through
others. I have read well over 1,500 books. I read daily. I had
nothing else. Originally, I was fascinated with history, black
history. In school we read about George Washington, Abra-
ham Lincoln, Christopher Columbus. We read about white
heroes, every black face was a slave, a nobody, unacknowl-
edged. Our sense of self-worth plummeted. I was shocked to
read about people like Frederick Douglass, W. E. B. DuBois,
George Jackson, Huey Newton, Angela Davis, Harriet Tub-
man, George Washington Carver, James Baldwin, Cornel
West, and so many more. I felt like I found a treasure. I was
never taught about these things in school! I moved on to
read about Socrates, Plato, Marcus Aurelius, Freud, Viktor
Frankl, Frantz Fanon, Che Guevara, and so many more.

I went on to novels of every kind—I went from *[nonfiction]*
books by Robin Kelley, Malcolm X, Marcus Garvey, Eric
Williams, George James, Cheikh Anta Diop to almost
every new novel on the best-seller list. I quickly learned
that reading is a very expensive habit. While some prisoners hustled money for food at the commissary, I spent
mine on books.

> Whenever my mother sent me money, I would
> spend it ordering writing supplies and books
> on various subjects to make up for my lack of
> education.

Time taught me to ask the question, If my anger comes from pain, where did my pain come from? The answer: It came from love. It came from what we love or who loves us. That meant that even in my anger, it had roots of love. My anger could be used as a motivator, either constructively or destructively. I chose to use it constructively so my family would not hold their heads in shame. Before the evidence about my conviction surfaced, people still believed me to be a killer. In time, I proved them wrong.

That's when I began using this environment instead of just existing in it. That's when I started observing the other prisoners. Most people tried to be my friend, some out of fear, some trying to tempt me, some trying to educate me. Like Innocent, who I write about in my book. He was also young. He was eighteen when he came to prison. But he would teach me things that I wasn't paying attention to. He would teach me how to observe the demeanor of other prisoners. For some reason, a lot of sexual predators in prison avoid interaction with other men. They see men as a threat. For instance, sometimes we would play basketball. Most of the sexual predators would rather stay out of the game. They didn't want to argue who was fouled, what guys fouled. That could lead to a fight quick in prison. So you would look at who took extra precautions to avoid any type of conflict. The majority of the guys who didn't play were the sexual predators.

The prisoners who sexually prey on other prisoners are usually not the ones who are in here for sex crimes. You know what the id is? That's your instinctive pleasure principle. It's kinda like, you take on a caveman syndrome. If

you look back at the cavemen, they didn't ask for something, they took it. If they wanted sex with a woman, they
didn't ask for it, they took it.

Here, the id runs rampant. I call it the Caveman
Syndrome because it's kinda like brute strength wins.
In prison it's not the intellect that counts. That's not
the respect factor. Brute strength is how you get respect.
Fear.

My instincts became so honed I could read a person's body.
I could read a prisoner's hands. Look at my hands. I got scars
all over my hands. It's from fighting, prisoners and guards.
I've had my hands broken, scarred, cut. I can read the other
prisoners by their hands. I could read a prisoner's body and
tell if they are willing to fight or not willing to fight.

When guys don't have an outlet to do something constructive, their minds become creative-destructive. They focus on
how to manipulate another person. I've seen guys get in
fights over chips or candy. There's no telling how far they
will go. Most of the times when guys fight, they take off their
clothes all the way down to their boxer shorts. Why? Often
someone gets a busted lip, cuts on their hands, etc. When
the guard sees blood on clothes, it means someone was fighting. If the guards find out about the fight, an investigation
takes place. During an investigation, everyone may not be
allowed to go to recreation for a few days. No one wants to be
punished for someone else's fight. We make sure if someone
is going to fight, well, they don't get us in trouble.

Then, the next thing you know, the guys in their boxer
shorts become a joke. Guys grabbing ass or doing this and
this, and getting away with it. One thing leads to another,

and next thing you have is a booty bandit. That's what they call it, a booty bandit—someone who will rape another man.

I've seen a lot of instances where after a fight and one guy knocks the other guy out, he will strip him. It's not to sexually mess with him. He'll strip him to degrade him psychologically. No one would ever do that to me. No, I don't think . . . [LAUGHING] If you look at my evidentiary transcripts, most of the trouble I've gotten into in prison has never been something concerning Nanon Williams. It's me standing up for the guys who've been abused, who've been jumped on. That's the whole point of my evidentiary hearings. Ask Morris. He'll tell you.

Morris Moon is one of Nanon's appeals lawyers. Morris says, "Nanon and I have a very strong relationship. I try to keep in touch as much as I can, though not as much as I'd like. We correspond a lot. He's a very personal person, easy to work with in the sense that he's smart, he's engaged in his case. He's an amazing person."

I started writing. First I wrote poetry on a roll of toilet paper. Later I wrote a book about life on death row called *Still Surviving*. My mother published it for me. Jazz encouraged me to write about the other men. I did. And my mom published a second book, interviews of the guys about to be executed. Jazz would tell me to focus on the battles inside these walls because the wrong people were dying. The memories of a man, the strengths that he had, the knowledge that he gave, the wisdom, that all dies with him. It never reaches outside where it counts, where it can have an impact with students or journalists, people who can make others understand what's happening. The more I wrote, the more I could show people who they were, instead of what they were judged to be.

In time I learned what I was standing for. You need to believe in something. Me, I just believed as long as they can't break me, on any level, I will retain some part of me, even though some of the things I was doing was stupid. Some of the conflicts with the guards, you know, they could have been avoided.

I want to have a clear conscience about what's right. That doesn't mean I always *know* what's right. In my mind I try to be right. There's no sense in me writing about things, then not taking a stand for what's right. In my mind I always try to be right—it doesn't mean that I am.

In 1996, Nanon started a prison newsletter, The Williams Report.

By writing I learned the difference between fear and respect. People say, "Hey, man, at the moment of my execution will you write about me, will you write my mom, will you write a story and send it to my daughter?" I do. As long as people feared me, I always had to watch out somebody would stab me in the back. Now, I got people watching *my* back. They'll say to a dude, "Don't bother him."

Everything here is personal, whether you like somebody or not. Because you listen to them scream, you listen to them talk, you listen to them play each other, you listen to them lie about all the women they had or all the things they accomplished. So everything here becomes personal.

For example, the guys used to get executed at midnight. (They changed it now to six P.M.) The night before, they are allowed visits with their family. Then they take them to Walls Unit, back in Huntsville, where they are executed.

The night before, the prisoner can request to speak with other prisoners. Right before an execution, it's always good to stay with close friends. They let us sit in a legal booth, similar to this one, and talk, maybe for a couple hours. Since I was writing, many of the guys would request me. I've had visits like that about fifty times, if not more.

I've had guys about to be executed call me for a legal visit and say, "I just want you to know, man, hey, man, I've always liked you, even though we used to argue and this and that." It makes me deal with their executions, even if I don't want to deal with them.

Sometimes they would let us have legal visits in the wee hours of the morning, two, three o'clock. Sometimes close friends could sit in the legal cage from maybe one to three, four o'clock in the morning. They can't sleep. They are writing last letters.

I remember a guy named Domingo. I couldn't stand him. All he used to do is cuss everybody out. And he would never go outside, so you couldn't kick his ass. He used to always talk crazy to everybody. But when he was about to get executed, I was the one he wanted to talk to because I wrote the newsletter.

One day the guard came and said, "You got a legal visit with Domingo Canto. Do you want to go?" I was still young, about twenty-four, twenty-three. I didn't want to see him. But it's kinda like peer pressure, 'cause the guys were saying, "Well, are you going to go?"

So I was, like, "Yeah, I'm going." I really didn't want to go, because I thought the dude might want to cuss me out or whatever. But then, the other guys might say, "He must be scared to see the dude," or something.

"Yeah, I'll go."

When I went down there, I said, "What you want?" I didn't want to hear nothing he had to say.

Domingo said, "I know I did a lot of things, and I don't know how to deal with it, but I'd appreciate it if you would write about me." And he was humble. He was preparing to die. He would be executed in less than twenty-four hours. He was scared. This was his way of reaching out. He cried and said, "Hey, man, I see you down there trying. Hey, man, everybody don't do that. Write about me if you can. Write something to get people to understand what's happening. Don't just write the bad things, let people understand." And I don't know what to write about him, I never had nothing to do with the dude.

Right before an execution it's so quiet. Not here, not where I'm at now, because you have a lot of psych people here, people on medication. They'll scream just for the hell of it. But on most pods, from five to seven, we try to honor the man by giving him a moment of silence. The guys started that long ago. They give him a moment of silence. A lot of guys can't handle that. A lot of guys don't want to know when someone is getting executed, but when they hear the silence, it forces them to deal with execution. It makes them think about their own execution.

Just before Jazz got executed, I was in a legal cage with him. We sat in a booth just like this one, except we had steel-mesh wire all around. While I was talking to him, I was trying to be strong for him, but he was cracking jokes, laughing. He was trying to be strong for me. This was the day he was going to be executed!

NANON'S APPEAL

Early on, I didn't care about the appeal process. Besides, who would believe me? There's a difference between saying something and proving something. How many people around here cry wolf because they don't want to die? Damn near everybody.

Meanwhile, the lawyers were working hard to get Nanon's case back in court. If there is new evidence, it's the appellate lawyer's job to get the court to hear it. When Nanon met his new court-appointed attorney, Helen Beasley, who was born and raised in England, he was struck by her beauty and her soft, thoughtful demeanor. He said that he became nervous when the guard left them alone together.

Was I supposed to sit or stand, follow what she did next, or what? I wanted to behave like a gentleman, but maybe I had forgotten that, too? Gradually, after speaking about legal matters, all I could do was be myself.

Helen called for an independent test of Vaal's .22 and the bullets. Until she made this request, that gun had never been tested, even though it was the only weapon the police actually had in their possession. Before the gun and bullets were released, a prosecutor asked Robert Baldwin, the state's ballistics expert, to test fire it himself. When Baldwin tested the gun, he realized that he had made a mistake. The bullet taken from the murder victim's head had been fired from the bottom barrel of the .22 (Vaal's gun), not the .25 (Nanon's gun).

Nanon often refers to Helen as "an angel fallen from the sky to fight for me." He wrote in his book, "I wanted to believe this. Even more touching, Helen seemed to believe in me. She believed in me!"

1998

Nanon returned from another stint in solitary. Two of his friends had already been executed, Rogers-El and Da'Oud. Life couldn't be more bleak. But then, things happened.

Nanon's mother flew to Livingston, Texas, to break the news in person. She said, "There's been some new development concerning your case. Your attorney said that you've been granted a very important hearing and that you may be transferred back to Harris County Jail within the week."

In September, Nanon was transferred back to the Harris County Jail, the very jail where, years earlier, he had met death row prisoners talking about their own appeals. It's interesting how one's life can make a full circle. At the hearing Nanon describes Helen as "smartly dressed in a conservative suit," while he had on an orange Harris County Jail jumpsuit that made him "look like a carrot."

Nanon's family and friends were present when Helen carefully presented the case to the judge. Nanon says, "As the hearing ended, I was allowed to hug my mother, my grandparents, and my supporters. I was coming out of the courthouse. My mother was hugging me, and I wasn't used to someone touching me, not gentle. I felt nervous. I felt out of place, even though it was my mother. I didn't know how to behave. I was shaking."

Thanksgiving, 1998, one of the boldest escapes in Texas history took place in the Huntsville prison. Seven death row prisoners made dummies from cloth and tucked them into their cots, cut through a chain-link fence, and hid out on the prison's roof. Around midnight the guards saw movement on the roof. Six of the prisoners were immediately captured, but one got away. A few days later, there was news that a body had been discovered in a creek a mile or so from the prison by two off-duty prison guards who said they were out fishing. It was the seventh prisoner.

Because of this attempted escape, the inmates on death row, including Nanon (who by now was back in Huntsville awaiting the judge's decision), were moved to a super-maximum-security prison called Polunsky Unit, in Livingston, Texas. Executions continue to take place in Huntsville, though, in the area called Walls Unit.

This place is designed so that everyone is in total and complete solitary confinement. I was one of the first moved. Why? I'll get into that. This unit used to be called Terrell, but it was changed. The guy, Charles Terrell, for whom the prison was named, had a conflict with having his name on a place where they kill people. He wanted his name removed from the prison. I guess Polunsky had no problem with that.

In December, the district court judge ruled that Vaal shot Adonius Collier. Although Nanon had failed to establish his actual innocence (because there was testimony from the accomplices that suggested he fired the shotgun), she recommended that he be given a new trial. The judge wrote her recommendation to the Court of Criminal Appeals. Appeals judges make the actual decision about whether there can be a new trial.

Morris Moon says, "Helen went to the court of criminal appeals with the judge's specific fact findings. She said, in effect, 'Here's why Nanon Williams should get a new trial based upon the court's findings.' In a one-and-a-half-page written order, the criminal appeals justices simply ruled that they disagreed with some of the trial court's facts and conclusions of law, without giving the slightest hint as to which ones."

Nanon was denied a new trial.

Everyone involved in Nanon's defense was flabbergasted. "I don't know how any rational person can look at that case and say he got a fair trial." Morris's voice rises in anger about the injustice. "The Harris County district attorneys have a very difficult time admitting that they are wrong. I think that's a large part of it. I mean, Vaal ended up serving four years!" Helen returned to England. Morris, Walter Long, and Mark Olive took over the case.

LIFE ON DEATH ROW

There are no other death rows in the nation like Texas's. It looks like a dungeon with cages and more cages of steel.

It's very hot. I put water on my bunk and just lay on it when I'm reading. Oh, man, it's hot back there. Then you have people throwing urine. It smells like shit when you walk in some sections. We are confined to a cell twenty-three hours a day. We are allowed one hour of recreation daily in a small cage. Alone.

We are fed three meals a day through a slot in the door. Every time we are taken out of the cell, even to the shower, we are handcuffed. Me, at times shackled as well. We have no TV. No phone. Nothing. We are allowed paper, pen, books, a typewriter (if you can afford the one they sell), a fan, and a small radio they also sell that has bad reception. Other than that, we have nothing. The food is always cold, overcooked, or undercooked. The vegetables are rotten, and the meat is called "mystery meat" because we don't know what the hell it is. Do we take classes? No. We're not even allowed to take correspondence courses.

This place smothers people with solitude. There is no camaraderie here, at least not like it used to be. Most prisoners suffer from sensory deprivation. There is no human contact. The setup is designed to steal one's will to live. We're all in permanent solitary. But we got different status: Level I, Level II, Level III. Your level is evaluated based on recent disciplinary cases.

On Level I, you get to have a radio, a fan, a hot pot to heat up water, books and magazines, as well as one visit every week. And you're allowed to go to commissary every two weeks and spend seventy-five dollars. I use my money to get typing ribbons. Most cost $8.95 now. I often buy twelve ribbons every two weeks, stamps, and a few other things.

On Level II status, you can only spend money for hygiene. You get two visits per month and recreation is four times a week. On Level III you can't spend anything. You go to recreation three times a week and get one visit per month. You can always have books and writing materials in your cell.

I'm on Level I now, but they put me in a pod with the psych patients. Sometimes my pod smells like urine and shit. And then you got the screaming. It would make every hair on your body stand up. It would shock you. When you walk to the back, it's like a football stadium.

Our minds become trapped. We flee reality. In many cases entertainment is found through outbursts of various kinds, verbal assaults, piss thrown through the slot when people walk by, paper spears are thrown through the screen. I had to get used to it.

When you thrust people together with no constructive outlet, creative minds become dangerous. You think of things that are destructive instead of constructive. The violence, it rises and rises. The guys try to create more shock every day.

If you throw a kid in the swimming pool to teach him how to swim, he's uncomfortable at first. But then, when he learns how to swim and gets comfortable, he does backflips, dives. Back here, when the guys get comfortable, that's what happens. Guys throw paper spears through the bars to hit the guards. It becomes a competition. People compete to see who can do the most.

Everybody is like that at F-Pod. Everybody. Imagine you got eighty-four cells. Just walking toward them, I'm telling you, it sounds like a football stadium. You got banging on doors every day, all day. A lot of people kick the door just for nothing. Cussing out guards. Arguing with each other. Arguing over anything. It's just their entertainment, and they don't even know it. So when you multiply that with everybody being emotionally unstable, imagine what the environment is like.

Everyone around me is Level III. They have nothing. They ask, "Why is he on this pod with us Level IIIs? Has he caught a disciplinary case?"

No.

I have my radio and things. Basically, they want the others to see that I have all my privileges. So imagine how it makes me feel being back there, knowing everyone is saying, "Well, he got a radio and this and that." It makes them kinda envy you. They know I don't care about the radio no way. They know that.

For a long time I was on the pod where everyone had their execution dates. That was hard for me. Everyone had a date but me. Everyone knows I'm writing, so they ask, "Hey, man, will you put me in the next issue? Will you help me?" I can't help everybody, so I had to tell some people, "Hey, man, I can't." It made me feel like I had to choose and pick. I didn't like that.

In F-Pod, where I'm at, there are two "management"

cells. They are cells within cells, steel within steel. I'm one of two persons in one of those cells. I don't know why. They always put me in such places.

I can't see or hear nothing. I can't see outside the cell. They're not supposed to keep me in the cell more than thirty days. I've been here eighteen so far. But I don't want out. I like the quiet.

I'm no longer used to quick movements. When I see a sudden movement, it's usually someone throwing spears or someone throwing piss on you, so I automatically move forward or back. That's because in my cell pod the psych patients might piss on me. Not that they're bad or trying to do something to me, it's their entertainment.

NO BENEFITS IN A CAGE

I'm Catholic, but I was raised not to eat pork. Mostly they serve pork, so I get beans on a tray as a substitute. I don't know what they do with the food. I can't see from this cell, but before I could see out when the chow cart was rolled in, the guards put the food on a tray and hand it to you through the food slot. Sometimes the guards have been shaking down the prisoners' clothes. Every time a prisoner goes to the shower, they shake the clothes down, under-wear and all that. Then they handle our trays. So imagine, they just got through searching somebody's clothes, touch-ing their socks, shoes, and then they take out the food and hand you a tray. No, ma'am! I eat the ramen noodles. I buy ramen noodle soups to keep me going. I can't stand them, but they cost twenty-five cents. I can buy twenty of them and it only costs five dollars. I make them in my cell with hot water. Maybe I'm just paranoid.

We have a whole lot of women guards. Imagine this here . . . now, be honest . . . if you was a woman guard and you was around me all day and you saw me stripped naked every day, taking me to the showers, you don't think you'd look and say, "Damn, he looks pretty good!" I would if I worked in a prison. Whether or not I'd say something to somebody, I'd still think, "Damn, she got it going on."

So even back here, you have a lot of relationships developing between the prisoners and the women. Many do. I wouldn't. I'd never do it 'cause I'm fighting for my life. Why would I want to have any type of relationship with one of these female guards? If you have sex with them or something and then they get caught, they'd say, "Hey, he raped me." Then you get a life sentence.

A lot of times you get advances by guards. Some of them write you under different names. For me, it's not worth it because my goal is not to be comfortable in a cage. It's best not to have the benefits on any level in a cage.

I sleep on a steel bunk. There's a mat, a little plastic mat, but after you lay on it for about a week or so, it gets used to your body and it becomes thin. I just lay on the steel, anyway. When I lived in solitary, that was part of the rules. As long as I was in solitary, I wouldn't have a blanket. I wouldn't have a sheet. By law I was supposed to, but that doesn't mean they'd give it to you. I'm so used to lying on the concrete, I'm just used to it. They give us pillows. They just took the blankets away 'cause it's summertime.

My goal is to be free. Nothing less. It's why I don't get used to having things they can take away from me and use as a tool to make me do what they want to do. It's why I don't care if they put me in a management cell. I don't care about going to the commissary. I don't care if I can go down there and buy Snickers or cookies. I don't care if they give me a mattress. I don't care if they put a light in my cell. I'm so conditioned to not having it, there's nothing they can do to me to make me stop doing what I'm doing now—writing. I don't need nothing from them.

You know what I love the most? Working with students and kids. Six classes from a college in Maryland read my book and wrote questions to me. I dream for something more than myself. I dream that change will come, even if my pulse never sees it. My last dream in life is to make my mother proud. That is why I write.

As crazy as it sounds, I wouldn't change anything about my life. I believe in things. I believe in what I do, in what I say. I'm willing to look in the mirror. I'm willing to learn, understand, and think past my own suffering. I could have become a professional athlete who had everything yet believed in nothing. I could have known what I was fighting against, but never known what I was fighting for. I hope you can respect that.

After the United States Supreme Court raised the age at which a person is eligible for the death penalty to eighteen, Nanon's death sentence was reversed by the federal district court. Six months later, he was moved from death row to Coffield Unit, a maximum-security prison.

Nanon's lawyers continue to work for a new trial.

E-MAIL FROM ONE OF NANON'S LAWYERS, WALTER LONG: Nanon's life sentence is forty straight calendar years before the Texas Board of Pardons and Paroles can consider paroling him. The governor recently signed into law a life-without-parole sentence. This has become the only option other than the death penalty for a conviction of capital murder.

CHAPTER FOUR
Hate Is a Killer,
Dialogue I

When Napoleon Beazley was seventeen years old, he killed Texas businessman John Luttig during a botched carjacking in Tyler, Texas. He confessed to the murder. Mr. Luttig's wife, Bobbie, narrowly escaped death. John Luttig was the father of Judge J. Michael Luttig, of the Fourth U.S. Circuit Court of Appeals in Virginia.

Two people witnessed the events of that terrible night. Cedric C. and Donald C. were accomplices to the crime. Later, they testified against Napoleon to avoid the death penalty.

In 2002, Napoleon was executed for the murder.

Because of his age, and because he had no prior record, the fact that Napoleon Beazley was given a death sentence triggered a national and international crusade against capital punishment. Napoleon was one of twenty-two men executed between 1973 and 2004 for a crime committed when they were under eighteen.

The Beazley family still lives in the house where Napoleon grew up, in a small town called Grapeland. His mother, Rena, is an appealing, no-nonsense woman with an earthy laugh and inviting smile.

Rena picked me up in nearby Crockett, Texas, and we drove to her home to meet her second son, Jamaal. She apologized that her husband, Ireland, couldn't join us because he was out of town on business. Even before this incident, the Beazley family were well known in the community. Ireland Beazley was the first African American elected to Grapeland's city council.

Rena refers to her son's act as an "incident." And after all these years, she still cannot understand how he could have done such a thing. "What are the odds that three country boys go out and kill the father of a federal judge? What are the odds in general that teenagers go joyriding on a weeknight? I can see them running around on a weekend. But on a weeknight? To get up and go to another city and shoot somebody? On that night? It's eerie."

But that, indeed, is what happened. Now two people are dead, John Luttig and Napoleon Beazley. What's left? The Luttig family grief. The Beazley family grief.

Inside their single-family house, Jamaal waits in the living room. Jamaal Beazley is big, *a soft bear of a man with warm, bashful eyes. He immediately gets up and wraps his arms around me. In spite of his generosity with hugs and kisses, it is not easy for Jamaal to express his feelings. He's a private person who has had to deal with a series of public events at a very young age.*

Jamaal has had to face the fact that the brother he so dearly loved and admired murdered another human being. He also has had to live with the reality that the state and country he also loves wanted his brother dead.

Jamaal and his family are left with so many unanswered questions. And memories.

JAMAAL: Love is worse than hatred. Love will tear you apart. Love will hurt your soul. I'm more solemn than most people, than a lot of people. If you lived through what I lived through, you'd see how hard it is to cope.

My brother was strong. He was athletic. According to some people he was very attractive. Smart. He was very well-rounded, very popular. Class president. Captain of the football team. In order for him to be elected president and captain of the football team, that tells you right there that he had a lot of popularity, even though this is a small town. I mean, there's nothing you can say bad about him.

We were eight years apart. I was his little brother. He was in high school, and I was in elementary. But he took me places—when he felt like it. He didn't want to hang with me all the time, his little brother, because I nagged. All little kids are nags. I cried a lot. Most little kids cry a lot. But he was my protector.

RENA: Napoleon was quite a bit older than Jamaal. He would have Jamaal crying quite a bit. [LAUGHING]

JAMAAL: You don't have to say that on tape, Mamma.

RENA: Now you know I don't know how to not tell the truth. [WE'RE ALL LAUGHING] That's just the way it is. They were typical brothers.

Jamaal wearing his Napoleon Beazley T-shirt
(opposite)

JAMAAL: I remember being chased by a bunch of older kids one day. He just stepped outside and they quit chasing me. That's because Nap was, you know, real popular. I remember all that vaguely. Most of my memories of him are later, when he was in prison. I was nine when Nap went to prison. He was seventeen.

The one thing I remember when he was arrested was there were police everywhere. I was looking outside my window as the police were going through our trash. Police going back and forth up and down the street. I wondered why are the police around here?

When Napoleon was in the county jail, I don't remember if I was shocked or what. I was such a little kid. I can't tell you what was going on. Later, once he was on death row, I visited him almost every week.

Mamma? Where was he arrested?

RENA: He was arrested at my mother's house in Crockett, the next town over. He was spending a night with my baby brother, who is a year older than Napoleon.

There was a caravan of authorities who came here. We saw the flashing lights, I guess about twelve thirty at night. I went out to see what was going on. They were searching the field across the street. They found guns in a bag, and they already had Cedric and Donald in custody.

The authorities informed my husband that they were going back to Crockett to pick up Napoleon and take him to Tyler *[where the murder took place]*. They picked up Napoleon, Ireland followed them in his car, and I stayed home.

JAMAAL: I was home sleeping, so Mamma had to stay here with me. I didn't know what was going on. I knew a man was dead, but I really didn't know what dead meant. I knew when Napoleon was in court, but I didn't know what court meant. Sometimes people do something bad, and it might be true, but you don't want to believe it, especially when there are no other signs of bad. Like, you wouldn't think Michael Jackson would do nothing like what he was accused of doing 'cause he does so many good things.

RENA: Napoleon was arrested June 1, 1994, and the trial was in February '95, after Napoleon turned eighteen. He was seventeen at the time of the arrest. He was tried as an adult. Jamaal didn't come at all. You were ten at the time.

JAMAAL: I went to one trial. I remember I kept putting money in the parking meters.

RENA: That wasn't a trial. What you went to was a hearing. That was after the trial—he was on death row at that time. Remember? He was in cuffs.

JAMAAL: The person that he shot was the father of a federal judge. Three Supreme Court justices knew him.

RENA: Napoleon showed no prior criminal record, an A student, popular. There's no way he'd be on trial for capital murder had the victim been anybody else. I don't believe it would have gone down that way. I know of a similar situation out of Smith County where the gal received a life sentence. The death sentence was revenge.

JAMAAL: If the victim had been a low-class citizen, Nap probably would have gotten three years.

There was a lot of publicity about his sentence. Even the Pope tried to stop it. I was interviewed for a Swedish magazine. Montel Williams wanted an interview. We was on Phil Donahue. This was the only case where a dude who was seventeen years old, class president, no criminal record, captain of the football team, baseball, track star, got a death sentence.

RENA: The judge *[the victim's son]* came here from Virginia for the trial. He offered to help the prosecutor. During the trial, the judge sat there and eyeballed Napoleon. He just glued his eyes on Napoleon, to the point where one of the deputies would stand between them, trying to block the judge's view of Napoleon in court. There was so much hatred in that courtroom. I never seen anything like it. I thought courts were fair and that the truth would come out. But this case was not fair.

We had no privacy with Napoleon after his arrest. All the conversations were monitored. We never discussed the incident with him. There were a lot of things we wanted to know, but we never found out.

JAMAAL: [AS IF SPEAKING TO HIMSELF] Sometimes people have mental breakdowns. How else could this have happened?

RENA: The brothers got state and federal sentences because they were also charged with carjacking. They're in for life, but no death sentence. They were offered a deal. Later, after they were sentenced and our investigators were brought in, they recanted their stories. But it didn't do any good.

E-MAIL FROM WALTER LONG, NAPOLEON'S LAWYER: Perhaps the best way to describe the brothers' sentences is to call them stacked state and federal sentences. By stacking the two sentences, one after the other, each brother would have to serve more than eighty literal years (no time off for good behavior, etc.) before being eligible for parole. The sentences are artificially constructed and beyond harsh, more than twice as long as life sentences given anyone else convicted of capital murder in Texas prior to 2005.

RENA: Before the incident, those boys were here all the time. They were even here the day of the arrests. The oldest had just quit college—I don't know if he dropped out or what.

Napoleon was a senior in high school. He only went to school a half day because he was on a work-study program. The oldest brother, Cedric, he knew Napoleon came home twelve-ish, so he'd come here and hang out. I'd come home and Cedric would be stretched out on the couch. Right here! And they would party together. They were here all the time 'cause they were partying all the time.

The boys knew I didn't approve of them hanging out here. I didn't approve of that. At the trial, Cedric said he was afraid of Napoleon. The youngest brother, Donald, said he was afraid of Napoleon, too. The night of the incident they said they were forced to go. Cedric said Napoleon told him he would kill him if he didn't go. You know two brothers are going to stick together. Common sense tells you they were all in it together. That's common sense. But the jury heard all this and embraced it.

At the time, I worked for the district judges in Crockett. I was a secretary to the judges, and I saw the way the courts were run. One judge told me what with Napoleon's record there was no way he'd get the death penalty. No way! You have to be the worst of the worst. Before a person is sentenced to death, the court asks three basic questions.

E-MAIL FROM WALTER LONG: The court doesn't exactly "ask" any questions. I'll paraphrase the law because the real instructions are filled with legalese and are very difficult to understand. In a case like Napoleon's, the court instructs the jury to make three specific, sequential findings:

(1) Will the defendant be a continuing threat to society?
   If the jury says no, the result is a life sentence, no death penalty. If the jury says yes, the second question has to be answered:
(2) When more than one person is involved in the commission of the offense, did the defendant foresee that a death would result?
   If the jury says no, a life sentence ensues, no death penalty. If the jury says yes, then a final finding is made:

(3) Are there sufficient mitigating circumstances that the death penalty should not be imposed?

If the answer to the final question is yes, a life sentence ensues. If the answer is no, the death sentence is imposed.

RENA: Initially, a judge told me there was no way he could get the death penalty. And after the trial, he boldly came into my office and said, "After all those bad things they said about Napoleon, they had no choice."

E-MAIL FROM WALTER LONG: The jurors had the choice, but their choice was called into question by the fact that Cedric and Donald gave testimony about bad things they alleged Napoleon had said or done, which years later they recanted as false. There is no question that the brothers' trial testimony affected the jury's choice of the death penalty. On appeal, the courts denied us the opportunity to put the brothers on the stand so that it could be determined whether their testimony or their recantation was the truth.

The bad things said at the trial and later recanted are described in Walter Long's clemency petition:

The C. brothers testified that Napoleon was remorseless following the offense. They now state that Napoleon cried all the way from Tyler back to Grapeland and that, immediately after Napoleon and Donald got back into the Probe

[Napoleon's mother's car] to make the return trip, Cedric had to take Napoleon's pistol from him because he was threatening suicide. . . .

Before the crime Napoleon said that "he simply wanted to see what it was like to kill or hurt someone." The brothers later recanted this statement, too. They both now say that Napoleon made no such statement before the crime, and that they felt pressed to introduce such statements out of fear that if they did not cooperate with the prosecutors to make Napoleon look bad, Donald at the very least would be exposed to the death penalty.

Walter Long believes that race was an additional factor in Napoleon's trial.

The prosecutors exercised one of their challenges against an African American prospective juror who belonged to the local branch of the NAACP, while choosing a white female juror, Maxine Herbst, who was (and currently is) president of the local branch of the United Daughters of the Confederacy and flies the national flag of the Confederacy from her house.

The March 1995 newsletter for the Tyler branch of the United Daughters of the Confederacy, in fact, notes Ms. Herbst's service at Napoleon's trial, remarking, "[W]e are all truly

blest to be in a country where we will be judged
by a jury of our peers."

Napoleon Beazley was not judged by a jury of
his peers. The prosecutors, furthermore, stirred
the nonrepresentative jury to think about Napoleon in terms of race. The prosecutors repeatedly exhorted the jurors to recognize that the
trial was "about" the white, upper-class victim,
John Luttig, who was described as an exemplary
human being and, at the same time, one of them
repeatedly described Napoleon in closing argument at the punishment phase as an animal
lurking about, looking for someone to devour.
The prosecution seasoned this Southern racist
image of the young black man as animal with
stories about inner-city influence on the defendant, raising fears in the white audience of pene-
tration of their bucolic world by gangs, drugs,
and ghetto culture.

Following the trial, one of the jurors com-
mented, "The nigger got what he deserved." His
then current wife gave us an affidavit in which she
attested that he harbored racist bias and that she
thought it would have been difficult for him to lay
aside his bias when deliberating on punishment.

A co-worker told us that the juror, a small
appliance repairman, would refuse to work on
the appliances brought in by African American
customers.

RENA: People thought he was dealing drugs. But nobody could prove that. The police officer who took the stand as a witness for the state said that he had heard rumors about Napoleon dealing drugs. But when he was asked why he never arrested Napoleon, he said he was fearful of his job because Napoleon's daddy was on the city council.

None of this information was substantiated. None! All rumors. Napoleon didn't testify on his own behalf. And Napoleon never spoke directly to the family. Knowing when to shut up is a gift from God.

JAMAAL: As I got older, I understood more. I know it sounds crazy, but Nap's situation made me respect my brother even more. When I was seventeen, I was wondering what I was going to do with my life. I didn't even know if I was going to college. Half the people go on to college because their mammas done make them go. Or they have scholarships or something. At around that age, Nap was already on death row. He had his execution date set. He had to cope with bigger things than going to college.

At seventeen I was surrounded by thirteen-year-olds to seventeen-year-olds. Nap, at seventeen, was surrounded by twenty-one- to ninety-nine-year-old convicts. He had to mature fast. He had to. Death row can make you crazy. You gotta have a strong belief in God. Nap had a strong belief in God and a strong belief in his family. When you build a house, if you don't have that strong concrete slab at the bottom, at the base, the house will crumble, even if

it is a good house. Nap grew up in a good, strong house.
And he was strong.

He wrote poetry. Here's one of his poems here on the
back of my T-shirt. I think our visits kept him strong.

We went down to the prison every weekend. We had
a two-hour meeting every Saturday. I think that helped
keep his head on. We did that for about eight years,
when I was nine to seventeen. He didn't really talk to us
about his being in jail. He left what went on back there
in the prison in the prison. You come from New York,
right? You don't want to tell me about the *bad* things
in New York. You want to tell me the *good* things in
New York. Same with Nap. But he couldn't tell me anything good because he had nothing good to say about
death row.

RENA: You were only allowed two adults at one time. Two
adults and whatever kids you bring along. I went to the
prison every week, and then everybody else would rotate.
That was Ireland's idea. Kids can get in until they are sixteen. At first Jamaal didn't have to be on what they call
"the list," the list of ten people who were allowed to visit.
Then, when he turned sixteen, he had to be on the list.
Jamaal would go on a pretty regular basis, unless he had
something at school going on.

We'd rotate in and out, except I would usually go and
somebody would go along with me. We always went in
twos. One of us might go to the bathroom or walk away to
give the other person a little privacy, but we would always

take advantage of the two-people rule because you only got two hours per week.

We would get in as many family members as we could. A lot of times I'd take one of my nieces. Sometimes I'd take friends.

JAMAAL: When we got together, we'd mostly talk about the band or football. I played in the band and was captain of the football team. That's pretty much what we talked about. Any time I needed advice, he would help.

He was interested in everything I had to say. He collected all the newspapers about me and the football team. He always told the other guys on the row to leave him alone, or he would get his brother to come beat them up. [LAUGHING] He would say "big brother" 'cause even though I'm his little brother, I'm way bigger than he was. The other guys who saw me said, "Yeah, man, your little brother is *big*! He's big!" It embarrassed me in a way. But it made my head blow up with pride. It made my head explode. Here they all were on death row.

In school I was outstanding because I was so athletic. And I made good grades. But outside of school, I didn't play with nobody. I didn't talk with nobody. I didn't go to parties. I had girlfriends but not to the point where we'd go out. Most of the girls I would talk to were from out of town because I didn't want to talk to too many girls in Grapeland. Anyway, half of them are probably my cousins. Most of the people in small towns are all related.

It was hard to tell people I had a brother that was on death row. Sometimes I thought they would just assume that maybe I'm a killer, too. Or maybe I'm just bad. Or maybe I'm just blah-de-blah-blah-blah.

It's not that I was embarrassed about my brother. Oh, no. I mean, like, I can't imagine I'd be embarrassed by him. Besides, it wouldn't matter whether I was embarrassed or not. Everybody knew who I was. Everybody knew who he was.

RENA: What I saw Napoleon do was torment himself. I don't know, maybe it was his sense of guilt. He would sleep on the concrete; he wouldn't sleep on the mattress. He had some bone disease in four teeth. He didn't take pain medication when they pulled those teeth. He endured that without medication. Like I say, he tortured himself.

He was mixed up at the time of the incident, but he was still basically very caring. During our visits, he would concentrate on you. He'd say, "Okay, tell me about yourself." It was all about us. That was Napoleon, he was always that way.

JAMAAL: Nap tried to redeem himself for what he did. But people don't want to hear that, they just want revenge.

Of course, there are other people that get into a bad situation just because they want to. And that makes it bad for the people who are trying to turn themselves around and redeem themselves. Hatred is a killer.

RENA: They were supposed to put Napoleon in Ellis I Unit *[in Huntsville]*. But then after the escape *[the Thanksgiving prison escape mentioned in the previous chapter]*, they decided to transfer everybody to a more secure facility. To do this, the police secured all the roads. They put police at each intersection. The prisoners were all shackled together, crunched down. They couldn't even walk straight up. And that's the way they rode, crunched down, from Huntsville to Livingston.

I didn't hear about this from my son. As Jamaal said, he wouldn't talk about prison life. He'd say, "I don't want to be here. Why do you think I'd bring you here?" So he didn't share any of that with us. All the other inmates would complain about the meals. There were times, when they were being punished, they'd take the hot food away and they'd get sandwiches. The inmates would complain. Napoleon never complained.

JAMAAL: When we visited him, we could never touch him. Even the last time. It was always through the Plexiglas. [JAMAAL STOPS . . . TEN SECONDS . . . FIFTEEN] The only time I touched my brother was at the wake. I guess I wouldn't consider that touching.

RENA: You never got to touch Napoleon, but I did. Several times. Every time we went back to the Smith County Court for a hearing, I got the opportunity to touch him. That's the county where the incident took place. I got to touch Napoleon only by the grace of God 'cause touching is not allowed.

Whenever he was taken to court, we'd be there. For the hearings he was allowed to change into regular clothes. I'd take him his clothes, and that's when I touched him.

About three or four times. The last two hearings he had to wear the prison gear, and I didn't get to touch him.

This tragedy didn't divide us a bit. I think it brought us closer. No one turned their backs on us. People clung to us and clung to him. We did trial issues on the media, we would get mail from all over, cards. People would point us out. Everybody was very warm. The whole community rallied around us. Not just here but all over. Churches were praying all over.

I couldn't go to Wal-Mart without being there for God knows how long. Everybody wanted to let me know... mostly mothers wanted to let me know... that... you know... "it could have been my child."

They did a huge story in Sweden. It was about twelve pages long. He'd get letters from people abroad and communicate with them in their language. And I don't know how he did it. He was awesome. I never met anybody like him. He would write to us in his regular handwriting. But he had a different handwriting when he wanted to impress the girls or something. It was beautiful penmanship. Beautiful. He was awesome. I mean, that was a waste. Killing him was a real waste.

JAMAAL: Napoleon's execution date was August 15, 2001. The day before he asked to see me. Only me. He only wanted to see me, but Daddy didn't want me to go alone, so he came, too. I don't remember what we talked about at all. I was in my zombie state. But I remember when it was time to go, he said, "Man, these people want me to die." And I said, "Man, I know." And he said, "Man, just keep your head up." And we both started crying. That's really all I remember. I can't remember nothing else.

He gave me all of his letters. He wanted me to take them home 'cause they was just going to throw them away.

I was walking out the prison with Nap's belongings. As I was walking out the door of the prison, some lady and some dude started attacking me with a camera. And here I just got to see my brother for the last time. I was leaving my brother knowing he was on his deathbed. I was trying to hold on, trying to get to the car as quick as possible, so I could calm down and have a moment of relief. I couldn't even take two steps out the door when this dude with a camera and this lady walked up to me with a microphone. And I'm thinking to myself, am I a celebrity or something?

I'm looking at these people, like, Man, could y'all just leave me alone? I felt I was going to start crying, break down in tears. I wanted to fight somebody, but I couldn't fight these people with a camcorder in my face. I was frustrated with the world, and I didn't know what to do. I didn't know what to do. I barely made it to my car.

By this time I was seventeen, about to turn eighteen. Man, it's crazy. It's real crazy because . . . if you think about it . . . I mean . . . my hand goes out to my brother, it really does. He had to sit there and think about what was going to happen to him at such-and-such an hour. He had to think about how they were gonna take him to such-and-such a place, and, man, I can't say it. [LONG PAUSE] Most people would just kill themselves. But my brother was tough, and my hat goes off to him for that. I don't know if I could have done it.

He told me to keep my head up and stay strong. He encouraged me to move on. The next day, the day of the execution, we were trying to drive down to the prison.

[JAMAAL'S GIGGLING]

RENA: We were trying . . . I was trying to get dressed to go, but I didn't have the energy. I still had my robe on. I had my makeup and my hair done. . . .

[RENA'S LAUGHING]

JAMAAL: And I was sitting down on that love seat over there. The phone rang, and my sister, Maria, answered. It was Walter Long. "Mamma, we got a stay," she screamed. But all I heard was a whole bunch of whooping and hollering. I seen the door opened. I don't know who opened the door, but CNN people rushed in with their cameras.

RENA: They were staked out outside. There was media downtown, media everywhere. *Everywhere!* The media by the house was dispatching their information out to other media. They were waiting on the word when they could come inside. You see, they were going to follow us down to Huntsville. So they were just waiting till we got everybody dressed for the trip. The word came out that we had the stay. I opened the door. I wasn't even thinking about CNN, or anybody, and all of a sudden the camera was right in the hallway where we all were. And we're screaming. We were just ecstatic.

JAMAAL: When I first heard the whooping and hollering, I didn't know what was going on. I knew that something happened, but I didn't know if it was a *good* happen or a *bad* happen. Then I saw my mom fall on the floor, crying. She was shouting hallelujah, so I thought, Okay, maybe that's a good thing. She's crying, but she's saying hallelujah. Then I saw my sister going, "Praise the Lord. Praise the Lord. Praise the Lord." Then I knew everything was okay, he had the stay.

RENA: And of course the media hung out the rest of the evening. Networks were coming in. Local TV stations came. And we were just, like, "Okay, please . . ." We were hungry. We hadn't eaten in days. And now everybody wanted to eat. We wanted to celebrate. So we asked them if they could just please leave.

The community itself . . . people were just coming in, not even knocking. In and out. The back door was open. The front door was open. People were just coming and going. It was one big circle. So many people in our house you could hardly walk.

JAMAAL: I was gone. I didn't want to deal with the media. I didn't want to talk to the neighbors. I wanted to be alone. I got in my car and went to the lake and just sat there. I can't remember what time I returned. But I just sat at the lake and looked at the horizon. I prayed and thanked God.

When people go to jail, they miss the stuff we take for granted. They don't get to see the sky and the birds, a lake. I went to the lake to make a blessing for Nap.

I'm tired. I can't really think of the words I'm trying to say. [PAUSE] It was less than a year after the stay when Nap was executed—May 28, 2002. Nine months. Ask my mother about this part because my mind's going bad. Mamma?

RENA: A lot of people could have stopped it. The governor could have stopped it. The judge could have stopped it. There were a lot of folks who could do it. They just wouldn't do it.

E-MAIL FROM WALTER LONG: I was on my way to Huntsville on the afternoon of May 28, 2002, in order to say good-bye to Napoleon, when I received a call from Chris Simmons's attorney in Missouri, informing me that the Missouri Supreme Court had just stayed Chris's execution date, which had been set for the next week. The Missouri court had stayed the date so as to wait and see if the United States Supreme Court's opinion in a case called *Atkins v. Virginia* (issued a few weeks later) would have an effect upon whether juveniles should be given the death penalty. We had been urging everyone from the trial court to the Court of Criminal Appeals to the Board of Pardons and Paroles and the governor to stop Napoleon's execution for the same reason. I returned to Austin, where I again went to the governor's office and vigorously argued that the equitable and just thing to do was to stay Napoleon's execution following the example of Missouri's carefulness. We also asked the Court of Criminal Appeals to reconsider its dismissal of our petition (which argued for a ban on the juvenile death penalty based in part on what we predicted *Atkins* would do) and grant Napoleon a stay, because the Court's sister high court in Missouri had considered our arguments valid. The Court of Criminal Appeals voted against us five to three. The governor ignored the plea. Chris Simmons won in the Missouri Supreme Court and at the United States Supreme Court, ending the juvenile death penalty. Napoleon was killed by the state of Texas.

In 1987, the Inter-American Commission on Human Rights ruled that the death penalty for juveniles in the United States violated international law principles of equal protection because of the arbitrary way in which it was administered between the states in our country. Absolutely nothing could be more brutally and unfairly arbitrary than what occurred on May 28, 2002.

JAMAAL: He was executed three days after I graduated high school. I went to my graduation. I was a zombie. I can't remember nothing about the graduation. I don't even know what I did with the diploma. I can't remember who was there. I can't even remember who gave me a graduation gift. I was a walking zombie.

RENA: The whole family went to the graduation.

Three days later, the whole family went to Huntsville.

JAMAAL: The day of the execution we didn't see Nap at all. We went back down there to Huntsville, to the Hospitality House, across the street, just to be close. *[The Hospitality House is privately run by a group of Southern Baptists. It's near the Walls Unit, in Huntsville, where the executions take place.]* He knew we were out there. He knew.

When this was actually going down, I probably wasn't any help at all to my parents. I was in my own little world. I was a walking zombie. I was just going through the motions, every day, all day, my mind wasn't there. I have no recollection of nothing. I can't remember who was at the Hospitality House.

To me, the people who did this to Napoleon are cold-blooded killers. And the people who sat there and watched him die? *Watched him?* They are cold-blooded, too.

People don't see it like that. They see it as, well, he's getting what he deserved. Me? I look at it as if, if they can sit there and watch it, then they can do just as bad a crime he was supposed to have did.

RENA: Walter called us afterwards.

JAMAAL: I can't remember who was at the funeral.

RENA: Napoleon never rushed into the next day. He would live in the moment. He'd say, "Let's get through today, first. You're getting ahead of yourself," and things like that. He always wanted to just stay with the moment.

Every day alive was a good day for Napoleon, even on

death row. He thought, Okay, some people want me dead, and they are right in their thinking. You all want me to live; you're right in your thinking. He gave everybody their own lead. He never tried to control anybody else's thinking, except through education. That was what he believed. Educate people. You show them a way. That's what he became about.

JAMAAL: Me, like I said, I became a loner. I like to stay alone. I worry that peer pressure can make you do stupid stuff. Then those same peers will turn their backs on you, and you're left in a bad situation. I think that's pretty much what happened to Napoleon.

RENA: I think I changed for the better. I think I'm a better person, a better friend. I don't know if it's because of the incident. It could be because I'm older, that's what's supposed to happen as you get older. I'm more aware of things.

To be honest, before this, I didn't think about capital punishment much. I never thought it would affect me. I always thought that death row people were the worst of the worst. And I thought if they were the worst of the worst, then let whatever happens happen. I didn't feel the need to challenge the death penalty. If a man is sentenced to death, he deserves it. Now I know this is not the case.

Newspapers reported Napoleon's final words: "No one wins tonight. No one gets closure. No one walks away victorious."

CHAPTER FIVE

Private with Our Grief,
Dialogue II

RICHMOND, VIRGINIA,
AUGUST 12, 1997,
10:45 P.M.

William Jenkins had just finished his second day of work at Bullets, a fast-food restaurant in Richmond, Virginia. He and two other employees were closing up shop. One worker was outside in the parking lot. The assistant manager was still inside when William approached the back door.

Twenty-three-year-old Charles Bass, aka Wild Child, was on the other side of the door. His two female accomplices, seventeen and eighteen, waited in the car. (The Jenkins family asked me not to use the accomplices' names because of their ages.) The plan was to rob the restaurant. The plan went dreadfully wrong.

When William opened the door, Bass put a semiautomatic revolver against his neck and told him to go back inside. William did exactly as he was told.

As they walked into the restaurant, Bass shot William in the neck for no apparent reason. He then ordered the assistant manager to open the safe. She did as she was told while William lay dying.

Meanwhile, when the restaurant worker who was still in the parking lot heard the shots, he called 911.

The suspects were arrested within minutes.

William's mother, Licia Hedian, is a midwife, and his father, Bill, was an assistant professor of speech and drama at Virginia Union University. Though Licia and Bill were divorced, Bill lived close by. (Bill has since married Jennifer Bishop and teaches in the Drama Department at Dominican University near Chicago.) William had two siblings, Mary, who was ten, and Paul, thirteen.

Paul is now a junior at Virginia Commonwealth University, majoring in computer science. Mary's in her sophomore year, studying interior design at Marymount University, also in Virginia.

The scene: Mary's dorm room. It's the day before Christmas break, and her roommate has already gone home. Paul, who is visiting for this interview, rocks on the back legs of the only chair in the room. Mary and I sit cross-legged on her raised bed.

Mary says, "I was getting an anxiety attack today. I was, like, I really do not want to do this. I do not want to do this. I do not want to talk about this in front of my brother. I have too many other things to do. I need to pack to go home. I need to clean my room. I don't know. It was overkill. But I'm okay about it now.

"I was willing to do this because, I don't know . . . I don't know, I wanted to do it.

William (opposite)

"Paul and I have never talked about this before. We don't know each other's side to the story. He talks to Mom, and I talk to Mom, and I guess we tell each other stuff, what we are feeling, but we don't talk about William."

MARY: I remember the night. I woke up in the middle of the night 'cause I was really, really thirsty. When I went to get a glass of water, I saw my grandmom cleaning the bathroom. Then I walked into the living room and found the rest of my family there. I said hi, in a confused way.

My mom said, "Go back to bed."

"Okay."

The next morning Mom and Dad took me into her room and sat me down on the bed. All I remember was Daddy talking the most. The main phrase he said was "something happened to your brother . . . he was killed," or something like that. He got really emotional. He said some other things to try and console me, but the only line I remember him saying was "and we loved him very much."

I thought, "What's going on?" I thought it was a dream and I was gonna wake up any second. This is all a dream. This cannot be real. And that's the way I felt for quite a while.

I got really depressed when I was twelve or thirteen. I thought, My whole life sucks. I was in Brookland Middle School, and I pretty much failed everything. I was not nice to live with. Mom and Paul remember my terrible teens.

PAUL: Yeah, I remember. You and I started fighting after William died, as a matter of fact. I had been sharing a room with William for about four or six months. That morning Mom and Dad came into the room about ten o'clock or so. I got up and offered them my bed. I don't know why. They sat down, and I sat down across the room at the head of William's bed. His blanket covered something. It felt hard and plastic. I shifted to check what I was sitting on. Pulling back the covers I saw it wasn't William's head so I put the covers back up and resumed my position. "Okay, no William," I said out loud, meaning, Okay I'm not sitting on William's head so he won't kill me when he wakes up. I'm safe.

I asked what was up. I was curious why Dad was in the room. That's when they broke the news to me that he had been shot at work. What's interesting about that moment was the dominant thought in my mind: Oh, my God, I just said that I thought I sat on William. That must have made them feel terrible. Then I thought, Why am I worrying about that? My brother has just died.

When they told me about William's death, they didn't have all the details. They didn't have a medical report. They only knew what the officer said, that William had been shot in the neck in such a way that he probably was dead before he hit the floor. They explained that a guy held a gun up to William's face, pulled the trigger, and the bullet went through his neck and lodged in his spinal column. In fact, the bullet went through sideways and split both sides of his carotid and jugular arteries.

Dad and Mom tried to figure out what they were going to do with all his things. That was one of the only times in my life that I saw Dad cry. He mentioned that he wanted to keep all of William's clothes because they still smelled like him. He broke down in the middle of the sentence. We didn't wash any of William's laundry for about six months after that. They were just lying in my room.

I only cried for William four times.

MARY: Four times? You're pretty nonchalant.

PAUL: Yeah, I know that now. I cried when they told me what had happened. I started to shut down the pieces of me that hurt. It was an instinct. It happened without my conscious effort. And the problem is that I shut down so many parts, there was very little left of me. What I mean is, I built walls, I put up a door. It was a one-way door. Or wall. I couldn't break it back down again. I couldn't open it back up. I closed myself down to the point where I had almost no emotions at all.

MARY: I noticed that.

PAUL: I could still feel some happiness, frustration-slash-anger. I could feel some weird sense of joy and complacency when I was satiated with food. But other than that, I basically went through all of my high school years without a soul. I had a lot of friends. I went to parties. But I had no soul.

What hurt most about William's death was that we had been emotionally distant except for the last two years. He had all these friends who would drink and smoke. And they got him into that for a time. I tried to hang out with William because he hung out with the cool people. He was a very advanced guy.

E-MAIL FROM LICIA, THEIR MOM: William's best friend was the son of a single mom who lived in the housing projects in Richmond. He went with a rough crowd. These kids had no hope for a future. They didn't expect to survive.

PAUL: I liked William's friends. They were nice guys. . . .

MARY: They were nice.

PAUL: A little misguided, sometimes. William was doing the adolescent "yes, this is my younger brother, please tolerate him" type thing. It's pretty typical. We had our good moments, but most of the memories I have of him are older-brother-terrorization type things. We would fight almost constantly.

William was the epitome of the firstborn child, and I was the epitome of the middle child. When he died, I knew I wasn't the middle child anymore. I was now the one everyone focused on, the one who did things first. That scared the heck out of me. Before, no matter what I did, William had done it before.

In my family, we are all brilliant. I have brilliant aunts, brilliant uncles, and brilliant parents. I'm not sure what happened with me.

MARY: That's a kinda weird thing to say.

PAUL: I'm smart, but I'm not useful.

MARY: [SHAKING HER HEAD AND CHANGING THE SUBJECT] I always think of him as older than me. I've surpassed William in age, and I still think of him as older than me.

William played guitar. He was left-handed, so he strung the guitar upside down, which I thought was ingenious. He was an artist. He was into a lot of things that I'm into now, which is what I get most upset about when I think of him. He's the one I could relate to the most, and I can't even talk to him about the stuff that I'm interested in now. We never had the opportunity to have that bond.

I feel I missed out. We could have done guitar together. He could have had his own apartment by now, and I could have gone over. Hung out. He was cool. I wanted my friends to meet him. I think he was very cute. He wore Mexican ponchos and flannel shirts.

PAUL: And I wore them after that, until I got too big. I still have most of the furniture that he used. The bed frame that he used is long gone, but I still use his mattress. It's very old. William used it in Tennessee without sheets so it's become prematurely aged from the skin oils.

After her divorce, Licia got a job as a midwife in Tennessee. They lived there for about two years before returning to Richmond.

PAUL: When we lived in Tennessee, the friends that William hung out with were Wiccans. They were largely into the occult. Wiccans are a modern religious cult that believes in witchcraft. A Wiccan is a person recapturing the ancient Druid religion. A lot of the Druid religion wasn't written down, so they're just trying to keep up with the traditions. And that's where you get your modern-day witches and warlocks. They're big nature people.

Some of them are a little odd and off the wall. I met a lot more of the innocent "I'm a happy, nature person Wiccan" rather than the group that William hung out with in Tennessee, which was more heavily into the spirituality of the religion itself.

One of his friends put an altar in William's closet. As far as I know, William didn't know about the altar for a day or two. My mom found it. She was perturbed. She confronted William about it, and in effect said that as long as he was living in her house, he would not do anything that is against her religion.

William had been experimenting with different kinds of spirituality at this time. He wasn't officially a Wiccan, but he had officially dropped his Christian roots for a time. He did eventually come back to Christianity.

One or two months before he died, William actually told Mom he was glad he was Christian and that he wasn't worried about dying because he knew where he was going to be if he died. That didn't help Mom too much when he did die. She was angry at God.

E-MAIL FROM LICIA: Part of the loss to me initially was my relationship with God. I don't mean that I abandoned Him or my faith—in anger or doubt. Rather, I can only approach God in prayer with what I am actually feeling and thinking, and I simply wasn't able or ready to talk to Him about it at first. I knew that if I once released all that was in my heart, I would be overwhelmed and might not be able to survive drowning in it. So the very thing that normally would bring me the most comfort, I could not turn to, at first. But when I finally did let it all out—including the "Why did you let this happen?" and "Where were you?"—I was immediately met with such an overwhelming sense of the Father's loving presence that it was like being wrapped in a warm blanket. If I did not know that William was even now alive and well in Jesus' household, I'm not sure I could stand it.

PAUL: The second time I cried was at the viewing.

MARY: I remember the viewing. First, it was just us as a family. We walked in and were all sobbing. We stood there and cried and cried. We didn't say anything. We just stood there.

PAUL: He was in a turtleneck sweater.

MARY: Yeah, because of his neck. It was weird because it didn't look like him. And essentially it wasn't him because he wasn't alive anymore. He didn't have *him* in him, in the body. I thought, What's the point?

The next day there was a public viewing, and that was

totally different. The whole atmosphere was different. I had a few friends from church there. They tried to distract me. We were running around, and they were trying to get me to smile. That was lighter, for me, anyway. I felt like I shouldn't have done that because it was my brother's funeral. I shouldn't have been happy.

PAUL: The third time I cried was at the actual funeral service itself. What was most touching for me was that most of his friends from Tennessee showed up. It was a very long drive. They brought along memorials to him.

MARY: Yes, that was beautiful. They had Domino's shirts because he used to work there, a four-leaf clover, some guitar picks, his drug rug—that's a Mexican poncho made from hemp, so I call it a drug rug.

PAUL: I wore it for many years.

MARY: I wore it after you. It was all torn up. It was special whenever I wore it. This was my private connection to William. I never told anybody.

PAUL: Somehow the body was transferred from the funeral home to Charlottesville, Virginia, an hour away. There was a service in my grandmother's church. She had bought burial plots for her entire family. Her children and grandchildren have burial plots there. It was a very sad thing.

I just wished after the funeral service that I could have

had a moment of privacy with William. I could feel him there. I could feel a connection that I would have liked to have explored. I think it would have saved me many years of emotional trauma if I had just been alone at the grave site for a few hours. It would have helped me move things along.

Instead, I shut myself down and was just a little, tiny person inside this little, tiny room, with no life and no exit. It was pretty bad for a couple of years. The only real sense of personal identity I had was when I was praying.

The fourth and last time I cried was when my childhood friend Trey was shot, perhaps a year ago. That triggered all of the grief from William's death, and the tears just poured out of me for a couple of hours.

That's gone now. I'm finished grieving.

NO DEATH PENALTY

MARY: I never questioned my parents' decision. No, never.

Dad's totally opposed to the death penalty. That's his whole movement right now, all about victims' rights.

PAUL: I'm pretty sure Dad's primary focus is that because it hurt him so much that William died he did not want to inflict that on any other person, like the parents of the murderer. The murderer was also someone's son.

MARY: That's how I see it, too. I mean, that's why I think the death penalty is a horrible thing. Everybody has

Mary

parents. Mom and Dad lost their son, and someone else was going to lose their son if "justice" was carried out?

E-MAIL FROM BILL, THEIR DAD: For religious and philosophical reasons, I don't believe that the death penalty is a viable way to stop crime. Never did. The prosecutor said that they were taking this case very seriously. This was a capital case.

No one would have blamed me if I just said, "Yeah, go get him."

But if you believe in something, you have to act on it or it's not worth believing in. I told the prosecutor that I didn't want him to do that. I think he was taken aback. He explained why he believed in capital punishment, and I explained why I did not.

I found myself in the bizarre position of pleading for the life of my son's killer. It was surreal.

Had we said we wanted the death penalty, Bass certainly would have been killed. Think about it, a sixteen-year-old white boy is killed on his second day at work by a black man who will be tried by a probably all-white jury in Virginia. Years later, I bumped into Bass's defense attorney and we talked about the case. He said we saved Bass's life.

Having seen how the system works in capital cases, I'm so glad we were not part of that system.

PAUL: I think Mom originally didn't want it on the principle of not seeking revenge. We've always been a strong Christian family. Strong Christian. Strong family. Not necessarily the strong Christian family archetype. She knew it was wrong to seek revenge, even though there were times she wanted it. Oh, she was pretty pissed for a while there. She still has lots of problems with depression at certain times of the year, around his death, around his birthday.

E-MAIL FROM LICIA: The commonwealth attorneys, to their credit, met with us and asked what our wishes were. We felt it was our responsibility that these people not hurt anyone else. I thought we had to make sure that happened.

If he *[Bass]* pleaded guilty, he would get life without parole, but not the death penalty.

They all pleaded guilty, so there was no trial. The case went right to sentencing. We got to make victim impact statements.

The terms of the plea agreement was that Bass could not ask for an appeal. This agreement helps survivors of victims because we don't have to keep going to hearings, which are very emotional and painful.

MARY: William's birthday was September 16, a week before mine. He died August 12.

PAUL: Christmas was difficult, seeing the rest of the family and all, and knowing that William wasn't here.

MARY: It's still difficult for me.

PAUL: Mom prayed a lot. She still holds the scars of losing her son.

E-MAIL FROM LICIA: I was in shock. I didn't feel angry at them, and I didn't feel I could forgive them. Only William could forgive them, and he wasn't around to do so.

Is forgiveness required? Is it reasonable? Is it possible? That's an issue the survivors of a victim must deal with.

PAUL: She eventually forgave the killers on some level. She wouldn't physically harm them if she came into contact with them. We didn't need revenge.

PAUL: William's death helped Mom and Dad's friendship.

MARY: They prayed together and became friends.

PAUL: It let her accept him as a person again. She knew she could depend on him if she needed him because he would still be her friend.

MARY: The person who murdered William was stupid. There was no point to it, and that really makes me angry. I mean, there was no point. Ahhhrrrr! I think it's worse to live with yourself after you've murdered somebody— unless you are some kind of heartless person. But somebody who knows it was a mistake, knows it was a spur of the moment thing, I think that would be horrible to live with. I mean, that's punishment in itself. I would want to die if I had killed somebody. I could not handle it, and I would feel like I deserved to die.

I'm sure he regrets it. Not because he got caught or because he's in jail. He has to live with that for the rest of his life. I think that's punishment enough.

PAUL: Mom once said that seeing the murderer in court made things easier in some ways because now she had a face to hate. She had a face to put all her feelings of rage and anger on. It made her want to see him dead. After that she did not want to go to too many hearings. But she went. I think she wanted to see it through to the end.

MARY: Nobody told me when the hearing was going on. I didn't know anything. I didn't know if there was a trial. I was totally oblivious and in my own world.

I understood what death was. I knew what murder was. I knew someone did something horrible to my brother.

TWO TEENAGE GIRLS

E-MAIL FROM LICIA: At the hearing, the only family that showed up was that of the eighteen-year-old. And she was the only one who showed remorse. The seventeen-year-old didn't cooperate until they were about to go to trial.

Bass and the eighteen-year-old were staying at the younger girl's house. The younger girl had been in foster homes. She was an emancipated adult, living on her own. The other two were mooching off her. The gun belonged to one of the younger girl's boyfriends. She also drove the getaway car.

They drove around looking for someone to rob. Earlier in the evening she had cased Bullets.

When I was at the hearing, the thing that struck me was that they were the same age as Will. Here were these girls who were like William's friends. I thought, Can't we adults do better? I certainly feel that we as a community have failed. I don't want to sound like a bleeding heart liberal—I'm a Republican—but this is what I believe.

The eighteen-year-old got sixteen years, and the seventeen-year-old got eighteen years.

MARY: I think it is really unfortunate for those girls. I
don't see why they would have participated in such a
thing. It doesn't make sense to me.

PAUL: They got worse sentences than they deserved. The
younger one will be around forty when she gets out. She's
living in a tiny box till then. She probably has really bad
times, prison girlfriends, that kind of bad thing.

I feel sorry for the guy. I never met him, but I've heard
he's not doing so hot. The last I heard, he was extremely
sick because of the cruel environment that prison is. I
don't know if he has AIDS, but Dad mentioned that he has
tuberculosis and all kinds of bad diseases. He's losing all
his hair. Maybe he has cancer.

There is an organization that works to bring about reconciliation between victims and criminals. Apparently
Dad's trying to see him that way, but he hasn't met with
much success. I would like to let him know that I don't
harbor any aggressions toward him. And I'm sorry he lost
his life by destroying my brother's life.

The thing with maximum-security prisons is that you
have to be on the visitors' list in order to be allowed in to
see a prisoner. They won't even accept letters from me. His
parents are apparently not capable of supporting the cost
of the trip, so they can't visit very often. They are a poor
family.

He threw his life away when he pulled the trigger. If he
hadn't, the other worker wouldn't have heard a shot, and
he probably would have gotten away with the crime.

MARY: Did they shoot him and then rob or rob and then shoot?

PAUL: They shot him and then robbed.

MARY: He was being cooperative, too.

PAUL: He opened the door because there was a knock on it. He probably thought the other guy who had just left was coming back for something. The guy with a gun comes in and demands all the money and then he shoots William. And the manager was so distraught over this that she tried to open the safe seven times. It takes her seven times to get the combination right. She probably thought she'd be killed, too.

MARY: It must have been horrible for her.

HURT PEOPLE HURT PEOPLE

MARY: Dad talked about William's murder all the time.

PAUL: He wrote a book about it, *What to Do When the Police Leave.*

MARY: I haven't read it—my confession.

PAUL: He spent almost every waking moment working on the book.

MARY: Writing the book. Revising the book. Republishing it. It has so many different editions. I think it was important for him to feel like he's making a difference because of this tragedy.

PAUL: After Dad's book came out, he tried pretty hard to get us to read it. He believed it would help us move on. We're not private with our feelings, but we're private with our grief.

MARY: Yes. Exactly.

PAUL: I approached the book seven or eight years after William died. I read the first chapter. It brought back memories of William's death, and I started getting ready to come to terms with it. I felt that it might be a useful tool. I actually read it the week before my friend Trey died.

MARY: I always wanted to read it, but I never got around to it.

PAUL: It's not really high on our list of fun things to do.

MARY: Right. At first I thought Dad's talking about it was more about his guilt for not being there after the divorce. But now I honestly don't think it was about that at all. I don't think it ever was, but that was what I felt for the longest time. That's more about my anger.

MARY'S ANGER

MARY: It started with William. His death brought this whole new movement into Dad's life. After William's death, I felt that my dad wasn't there for me. I felt that he wrote the book to make up for not being there. He was trying to convince himself that he was a really good dad. All the focus was drawn to William. It really pissed me off.

PAUL: Dad wrote the book to find closure and to honor William's memory. He also set up the William Benjamin Jenkins Trust Fund, but I'm not sure what it does.

His book got published, and people started inviting him to speak at different functions. He thought that this would be a good thing to do. . . .

MARY: But I think it led to the breakup of his marriage to Elise, his second wife. I loved Elise. I blamed Dad for the end of their marriage. Maybe his not being home affected her like it affected me.

Elise handled William's death differently. She isn't like Dad. I don't think she appreciated him exposing their lives. She was one of those people who wants to move on with her life and doesn't want to think about the past. The past hurt her. Elise was close to William. She was close to all three of us because Dad remarried while we were all young—

PAUL: We did enjoy Hanukkah.

MARY: She's Jewish, from New York. I still see her, and we're planning to go shopping this weekend. I went up to New York and stayed with her family.

Then, in 2001, Dad got a new job and moved to Chicago. And that led to his marrying Jennifer, who had two daughters who get to live with him. I'd call my dad and say, "Why? Why are you with them and not with me? You're my dad! It's not fair." My anger about losing William shifted to him.

I would have to travel to Chicago to see him. And the only time he would come down to see us was when he had a conference to go to. "Well, I have a conference, let me stop by, let's get together." It was, like, I'll make a pit stop to see my daughter. I got really, really angry. It was horrible, but it was typical teenage stuff. I'm okay about Dad now.

Jennifer's two girls were eight and ten. I was fourteen. I never had sisters before. They're really sweet and I love them, but it was hard to get used to the idea of having sisters who you don't spend time with. I saw them over Thanksgiving. Now they are older and I can relate to them more. They're starting to talk about boys, and I'm, like, doing the sister-type thing. I love them even more now.

PAUL: Dad volunteers at the Victim Impact Panel for the Cook County Juvenile Prevention Program in Chicago. This is a group of people who are survivors of victims. They talk about their feelings and experiences to teenagers who had committed certain types of crimes. The point of the victim awareness panel is to show what it's like to be on the other end of the knife. Hopefully it will evoke a change in some of them. They try to make a difference in the lives of these kids.

E-MAIL FROM BILL: We try to put a face on victims as a way to fight crime by beating it at its source. These kids have been victimized again and again and again. There's a slogan we use: "Hurt people hurt people."

PAUL: When I once went there with him, I heard all of the details about how William died. I knew that he'd been shot in the neck, but the way I had imagined it was different from the way it happened.

He talked about who the murderer was. The guy was just a kid who decided he wanted to knock over a store with a gun. The folks in the room could relate to this guy because they were all aggressive, malcontented youths, and many of them had performed robberies with a gun or knife. The guy who murdered William was one of them, a normal kid who decided to do something stupid and got caught. Now he would spend the rest of his life in prison.

Sitting there listening to my dad hurt. It opened up a lot of very old wounds. After that I actually got pretty introspective for a few hours and wrote out about three pages of a journal entry that I posted on the Internet when I got home.

I get tongue-tied very easily. It's more when I'm nervous

or dealing with an emotion that's powerful. So I needed some time to back off, be on my own, and get it written on paper. Normally everything I put on the Internet is stream of consciousness. I have a live journal.

Part of Paul's blog after that night:

I LIKE HAPPY FLUFFY CLOUDS. . . . I NEED A HUG:
i lack the ability to categorize today . . . it was . . . interesting and painful

after work Dad had a speaking engagement where victims of crime talk to parole kids and tell them our stories—so Dad, Jennifer and two other folks shared over an hour and a half . . . won't go into the details here—too painful—ask if you really want to know.

what amazed me was the strength Dad and Jennifer showed in their stories—i relived William's last moments and felt the grief all over again.

it was tough to just listen, i realized the hardship and difficulty in the life Dad has chosen and know that i'm not strong enough to follow in his path—mine lies elsewhere.

i love William so much. To spend another day with my Brother would mean more to me than

PRIVATE WITH OUR GRIEF, DIALOGUE II

anything. Try as i might i can't do anything but feel bad for his murderers. They're suffering so much now and i truthfully wish i could go to them and see . . . make peace . . . let them know i've forgiven them.

Sometimes opening an old wound hurts more than a fresh one, but allowing it to drain and air out can help it heal better than before. Hearing the story from Dad i got a better idea of what happened and how William died. I know it drains him to talk about it . . . he's healed up a lot better than i have though. Guess it's from airing his pain more often

Tomorrow is another day with new adventures.
I feel like curling into a hole for the rest of the evening . . .
God, i wish i had my music.
I need to curl into someone's arms BAD . . .

MARY: I went to one of Dad's talks at a college, too. I didn't want to go, but I had to tag along because I was in Chicago and that was what he was doing. He always brings a picture of William that he puts up before he starts talking. I was just sitting there and thinking, Why does he have to talk about this all the time?

I'm the kind of person who doesn't like to bring things up. I don't go out of my way to tell somebody my brother's died. If I make a comment that I had two brothers and now I have one, I'll just say one of them isn't here any-more. One of them got murdered. And I do it very matter-of-fact.

A couple of my friends know. That's only because I couldn't hide it. I'm not actually trying to hide it, but I don't want people to feel sorry for me. I don't like that. I don't like that kind of attention. When I was younger,

Paul

I thought people would look at me differently. People say, "I can't imagine what you're feeling right now. You're so brave and so strong." And I'm not, really. I'm living my life. The fact that my brother was murdered affects me, but I can live.

CHAPTER SIX

Dying for Legal Assistance: Roy's and Mark's Lawyer

When Bryan Stevenson walks into his classroom at NYU Law School, the students immediately straighten up. Perhaps it's the awe and respect students show for professors of law. Or perhaps there's something about this professor of law that makes the students pay attention.

In spite of his formidable credentials as one of the most celebrated anti–death penalty attorneys in the world, Stevenson is very accessible. A client on death row is afforded the same attention and consideration as a Supreme Court judge.

On this morning, Stevenson is relaxed and smiling, even though he was up most of the night planning an oral argument he will make before the Supreme Court. Wearing a burgundy polo shirt and gray slacks, he spends a few minutes fiddling with the overhead projector. "Oh, are we ready to begin?" He looks up and smiles, bemused by his lack of technical skill with the computer's projector.

Stevenson talks about the merits of the case he is about to argue before the Court. His client is a drug addict whose veins are virtually collapsed. In order to insert the needle that will eventually kill him, the guards will have to dig deep into his forearm to find

Bryan Stevenson

a viable vein. It will be very bloody and very painful. The client said, "I don't want them to cut me, to torture me, before my execution."

This presents the underlying question Stevenson poses to the class: Is it cruel to have a guard with little or no medical training cut through a vein to insert a catheter? And if this is so, does it not violate the Eighth Amendment?

Stevenson goes on to describe just how cruel executions can be. "There are accounts of botched electrocutions that are really troubling. Heads on fire. Eyeballs popping out. Defecation. People urinating on themselves. Burning. It's very ugly.

"Because of the toxic gases, the gas chamber is especially dangerous.

To avoid this, a person came up with the lethal injection. Injections appear to be painless. They're not." The same drugs were once used to perform euthanasia on pets. They have been banned by the American Veterinary Association because they were too painful.

BRYAN: I hate violence. There is so much needless, senseless, misguided violence. For me, the gratuitous violence of executing someone, or abusing someone in prison, is very, very troubling. Until we do something about poverty, about hopelessness, about despair that feeds violent behavior, we will all be at risk. I'm angry that we tolerate this risk.

I come from a religious family. I believe in redemption. I believe all human beings are valuable and should be treated with dignity.

I grew up in Delaware—rural, southern Delaware. My dad worked in a food factory. My mom worked on an air force base. We lived in a poor, segregated area.

When my parents were young, there were no public high schools for African American kids in their community. My father had to go to Wilmington, about eighty miles away. Back then, lawyers came in and applied the law based on the case of *Brown v. Board of Education*.

This opened white schools for me. Both my parents encouraged education, but no one in my family had gone to college. My mom had always wanted to go. In fact, after I went to college, she went back to school and ultimately got a college degree. She was in her sixties. I have a younger sister and an older brother. My brother and I had athletic scholarships. Mine was part athletic and mostly academic. I went on a soccer scholarship, oddly, even though I played baseball and basketball in high school.

When I was sixteen, my grandfather was murdered. He was eighty-six. He was poor. He was frail. He lived alone in a high-crime area in Philadelphia. This made him very, very vulnerable, a good target. Two young men broke into his apartment, stole a TV, and stabbed him to death. They were arrested and spent some time in prison.

That experience was very difficult for me. It was really devastating. I was not in any way consoled or comforted by the fact that we take the people who commit crimes and beat up on them. What it made me do is seek a profession where I could do something about the causes of violence.

I became interested in criminal justice, and race and poverty issues. After college I went to Harvard Law School, but I didn't know whether I wanted to practice law. After my first year, I also went to Harvard's school of government. It was an interesting experience, but I didn't see policy work as something I wanted to do.

During my second year at law school, there was a course that allowed students to spend the January term working with a civil rights group in the Deep South. I signed up. They sent me to what was then called the Southern Prisons' Defense Committee in Atlanta, Georgia. *[It is now known as the Southern Center for Human Rights.]* The group worked exclusively on death penalty and prison issues. I was very affected by the cases I worked on. I saw people who were literally dying for legal assistance. They were so badly treated, so horribly represented. Even with only one year of law school under my belt, I was able to provide more legal assistance than they had been getting.

My first case was helping a sixteen-year-old girl from Mississippi who was charged with murder. She had been in a relationship with an older man, a twenty-year-old airman from one of the military bases in Mississippi. When she got pregnant, he would have nothing to do with her. The young woman had an abortion. She became depressed and took up with another young man, who was seventeen. One night they got drunk. They went to the airman's house. The seventeen-year-old got into a fight with the airman and killed him. When the girl and her boyfriend were arrested, he said *she did it*. She insisted she had nothing to do with it, but because he gave the first statement, he got a deal. The girl went on trial, was convicted of murder, and sentenced to death. This was in the early eighties. She had horrible representation. Even her lawyer said she was guilty. Ultimately the sentence was reversed.

Cases like that one made it pretty difficult *not* to respond to people who have been condemned. I felt that I had to help people who are rejected by society the way death row prisoners are rejected by society. I had to represent them, especially since I believe that most people who end up on death row are there because they are poor and they are black. It's their identity, not their crime, that puts them on the row.

That summer, before my third year at law school, I

returned to the project and worked as a summer intern. Then, when I graduated, I started working at the institute full time.

Alabama had no institutional services for people on death row, no public defender system. There were a lot of problems in the state, a lot of race problems. The Southern Prisons' Defense Committee represented a bunch of prison conditions cases there. In addition to death penalty clients, I handled cases that had to do with prison conditions.

There was an outbreak of suicides and beatings in the prisons. There were prisoners who were epileptic and not provided with adequate medication. They were subjected to pretty horrible practices and medical procedures. I worked on those kinds of cases.

I was doing more and more work in Alabama and concluded that an institution for death row cases of indigent people was needed. I started the Equal Justice Initiative of Alabama *[EJI]*.

In 1989, I went to Alabama to get the project off the ground, expecting to go back to Atlanta. As I unpacked, a call came in from a man in prison. He said he was going to be executed in thirty days. I said, "I'm sorry, I'm not set up yet." But then, the man had no effective representation. I had to do something. I took his case, but he did not get a stay. Before he was executed, he said, "It's been so strange. More people have asked what they can do to help me in the last days of my life than in the last nineteen years of my life." And then he was executed. What does it mean to marginalize a person for so many years and then execute him?

The folks I work with often have a real sense of abandonment. This creates a relationship with me that is very intense. The guys on the row taught me an important lesson: Each of us is more than the worst thing we've ever done.

It never dawned on me that helping people who have done something wrong is a bad thing. My orientation has always been that injustice anywhere is injustice everywhere, as Dr. King would say. This includes bigotry and discrimination.

GOOD ADVOCATES

Is EJI hated? Respected? I think there's probably a lot of both. There are certainly a lot of prosecutors who feel like we are just horrible people. Some are threatened by what we do, who we are, what we say, because it challenges their control of the debate, of the dialogue. At times they react very angrily to our presence. We definitely get that a lot.

We try to be good advocates. We try to make our pleadings clear, articulate, and well defined. And, you know, by persisting in making the state do what the law requires, I think there's begrudging respect on the part of some judges.

We also get prosecutors, judges, and politicians who appreciate how unfair the system is, how out of balance it is. They say, "You know, it really isn't fair the way people are being warehoused and processed through the system. It's good you are trying to confront that. I can't say that publicly, but privately, I think what you do is good."

We have a lot of support in communities of color. They feel the injustice of the system so much more comprehensively.

VICTIMS

I think a lot about victimization. I'm troubled by the fact that we don't respond well to people who are victims. The people who lose loved ones in these cases just break my heart. I can identify with the sheer horror of having someone in the family killed. But I don't think we should respond to that by executing people, or by feeding this violence by saying now we have the right to hurt somebody else. I think we've got to get to a point where we see *all* aspects of victimization.

The trial process is very hard on a victim's family. They have to attend every hearing. They have to relive the crime over and over again.

We try to help family members of the victim understand that if they have questions, if they have concerns, we will address them. We tell a victim's family what's happening with the case. Obviously our primary obligation is to protect our client, but I feel there is an important dialogue that can take place between us and the victim's family.

We try not to lose sight of the fact that any crime that involves a death sentence is usually a crime that is horribly tragic and deeply regrettable and creates a lot of pain before anybody ever gets to court. I certainly have a continuing sense of that based on my own experience with my grandfather's death and other instances where my family have been the victims of violent crimes.

But I reject the view that the world is divided into two sections: the victims of violent crimes and the offenders. Some of the offenders we are working with are people who have horrible, horrible losses as a result of violent crimes.

The second part to this is an atmosphere that's created where the surviving family member is pushed to seek the death penalty. One of the real perversions of the death penalty is that we made it some kind of blue-ribbon test for *who loves their loved one the most*. This implies you are somehow less committed and less caring if you do not fight for an execution.

The whole point of our system is that if you lose a loved one to murder, you should not have to pay the burden of making sure justice is appropriately provided. I think that's unfair.

Can an execution change one's loss? Finality can still be achieved without the death penalty. One mother of a victim told me that she thought she would feel better after an execution. But she didn't. She still didn't have her son.

There's a wonderful coalition of people who have lost

loved ones to murder. Parents. Spouses. Siblings. Children. They've organized themselves into Murder Victims' Families for Reconciliation, Inc. The group advocates reconciliation and is adamantly opposed to the death penalty.

On the other hand, there is a movement floating around that the death should be as painful as possible, as brutal as possible, as ugly as possible as a way to deter crime. The death penalty does not deter crime.

DEFENDING CLIENTS

I think you see in Mark and Roy two young men who in a lot of ways typify the young people that I've represented over the years. They're needy. They struggle with themselves. They are undeniably human. They are undeniably youthful in their desire to be complete human beings. They have literally grown up to become different people from who they were—physically, emotionally, psychologically. The challenge to represent them has been a difficult but engaging one. It's wondrous to see that an act that condemned them to prison can be overcome.

In fact, the sentence we *[the state]* impose is not intended to only be about the severity of the crime, it's also about the character of the offender. The defendant is also a victim. Litigation work is typically organized around a person's history of victimization. It's about getting people to understand that there's a larger story than the event that brought the defendant to trial. This is important. Always.

Based on the data, it is the race of the murdered person

that determines the conviction. If the victim has high status, it is more likely to result in a conviction. If a four-year-old girl is murdered, what difference does it make if the mother is a corporate executive or a prostitute?

I'm troubled by that because this is another way to devalue lives of the poor, devalue the lives of people of color.

The sad part for me is that my clients come from places where they've experienced so much victimization themselves. You are looking at a community of people who have themselves suffered from violent behavior and crimes. My clients see siblings murdered, parents murdered, assaults, rapes. This becomes a way of life.

I'm angry about that.

"The ultimate weakness of violence is that
it is a descending spiral. . . . Returning
violence for violence multiplies violence,
adding deeper darkness to a night already
devoid of stars."

—Martin Luther King Jr.

AUTHOR'S NOTE

In No Choirboy, *I set out to learn about individuals involved in very violent acts. I visited maximum-security prisons in Alabama and death row in Texas, where I met people society brands "the worst of the worst," "the monsters." All the men I interviewed in the prisons had been teenagers when they were indicted for murder. Although not everyone featured here was a death penalty candidate, capital punishment is the book's central theme.*

The more I learned, the more I needed to know. As a nonfiction author, I cannot resist facts. I needed experts.

Enter Bryan Stevenson.

A number of years ago, Professor Ursula Bentele of Brooklyn Law School invited me to a panel discussion about the death penalty that featured Bryan as one of the speakers. His talk was fascinating, passionate, and inspirational.

Sometime later, I decided to write a book about capital punishment. Where to begin? The topic is vast. I thought that if Bryan Stevenson would consider helping me, even just a little, I could do this. Bryan did much more than just a little. He became my primary source of information.

After attending a remarkable seminar at Brooklyn Law School called "Capital Defender and Federal Habeas Clinic," taught by Professor Bentele, I audited Bryan's class at New York University Law School, "Capital Punishment Law and Litigation." There I learned that Alabama and Texas had had the largest number of juveniles sentenced to death in the country. I knew where I had to go.

Bryan opened doors, no pun intended, to two of his many clients—Roy and Mark. As things progressed, the book began to take shape.

Bryan also suggested that I call Jim Marcus, then the director of the Texas Defender Service. Jim introduced me to lawyers Walter Long and Morris Moon. They arranged for me to meet their clients, Nanon Williams and the Beazley family.

Although I was often tempted to stress certain themes—the symbiotic relationship between politics and the death penalty, the economics of a death row sentence, the complex Kafkaesque rules and regulations in the appeals process—two questions recurred: "Are you the sum total of your worst acts?" and "Are we able to determine, justly, what punishment people deserve for their worst act?"

RULES

The lawyers asked me not to talk to their clients about the crimes that sent them to prison. In many instances, litigation is ongoing, and they did not want to compromise their cases. Since our conversations are not privileged, I could be called as a witness for the prosecution. I was free to ask anything about the clients' feelings and childhood, and what prison life is like. Everything about the crimes comes from court transcripts, newspaper articles, and my interviews with the lawyers.

Allan B. Polunsky Unit, Livingston, Texas

The prisons had a few rules, too. Mostly they involved what I could bring to the interview. In Alabama, I had unlimited time with the prisoners. I could use my tape recorder, but no camera. In Texas, I had limited time with the prisoner. I could use a tape recorder and camera as long as I had the prisoner's permission.

Both prison systems had strict dress codes for all visitors. Alabama: no solid-white clothing (because the prisoners wore white uniforms), no see-through clothing, no short skirts. Texas: all of the above with an addition—no open-toed shoes. My wallet, money, personal items, and cell phone had to stay in the car. I suspect that the parking lot of a maximum-security prison is a pretty safe place.

MANY THANKS

I would like to thank Ursula Bentele, Bryan Stevenson, Walter Long, and Bailey Kuklin for reviewing several drafts and advising me on legal issues. Professors Susan Herman and Margaret Berger at Brooklyn Law School also took time to explain confusing legal principles. Aaryn Urell and Lee Eaton at the Equal Justice Initiative of Alabama assisted in the Alabama section of the book. The guards and prison wardens, especially Michelle Lyons at the Texas Department of Criminal Justice, were supportive and helpful.

In spite of expert advice, mistakes can slip through the cracks. Any errors are entirely mine.

Throughout this four-year project, my enthusiastic editor, Kate Farrell, kept my spirits up and the legalese down. Judy O'Malley started the project when we talked book ideas during one of our long, delicious meals. Author and friend Elizabeth Levy also read the manuscript and helped me become a better writer.

Jennifer Bishop-Jenkins, a board member at Murder Victims' Families for Human Rights (MVFHR), introduced me to her stepchildren, Mary and Paul. Jennifer, herself the survivor of the murder of her sister and her sister's family, met Mary and Paul's father, Bill Jenkins, at a MVFHR conference for murder victims called "Healing the Wounds of Murder." They married a year later. Sometimes there is a happy ending.

My deepest appreciation and thanks go to Roy Burgess, Mark Melvin, Nanon Williams, Rena and Jamaal Beazley, and Paul and Mary Jenkins. They bared their souls and opened my heart.

"EACH OF US IS MORE THAN THE WORST THING WE'VE EVER DONE."

—Bryan Stevenson

Nanon M. Williams Update

Since 2005, when Nanon left death row, he has continued to study, write, and work on reversing his sentence.
Throughout the years, his letters to me have been filled
with reflections that range from high hopes to downright
despair. Here are a few excerpts.

Dear Susan,

*I have quite a lot to write to you! However, today is Sunday
and all the NFL football games are on. It's one of the few
days of the week that for a brief moment (and I do mean
brief) I can forget about everything around me. Anyway, let
me address your questions.*

*Since I left death row, I've taken fifty-eight classes. I
have a college degree in Liberal Arts & Science and just
signed my graduation papers for a Bachelor's in Behavioral
Science. Since I'll graduate with honors, I've been offered a
partial scholarship to obtain my Master's in Literature &
Humanities. Please mention this because it is very important.
It shows others that despite overwhelming odds, we can still
achieve great things.*

In 2012, Nanon Williams was excited about a new trial. Earlier, a district court held a hearing and granted Nanon relief—meaning, granted him some kind of remedy to his situation. Family, friends, and attorneys were hopeful that a new trial would reverse Nanon's sentence and maybe, just maybe, he could be released on bail.

During this period, Nanon's letters were filled with optimism and confidence. He upped his courses, taking as much as he could as fast as he could. Sociology. Philosophy. Women's studies. His letters were filled with pages and pages of opinions and questions about music, art, and politics.

Then the roller coaster ride began.

Nanon's Case

As far as my case, in 2010, a federal district judge ordered my release or a new trial in 180 days.

Everyone was optimistic because new and sophisticated forensics proved that Nanon was not the shooter. But a three-judge state panel denied Nanon the relief. Even though three state and federal judges had already granted new trials, this higher court panel denied their rulings.

Nanon's attorney requested a rehearing *en banc* (a legal term used to refer to a case heard before *all* judges of a court, rather than by a panel selected from them). But the

"Petition for Rehear *En Banc*" was denied with no explanation. Nanon's sentence would not be reviewed. Then the United States Supreme Court upheld that ruling.

Dear Susan,

I know you worry about how writing about me might affect my case, but the truth is, it's pretty much over. I've won, won, won, and yet I'm still here. I am still in prison. I am still condemned to be a killer I never was. I still have a sentence that says I will die in prison. I may find happy moments, but I am not a happy person. If I do ANYTHING it's to help other men avoid becoming like me. Texas has more juvenile offenders certified as adults than any other state, and even if they are not life sentences, they get on average thirty years, forty-five, ninety-nine years, even for cases like robbery. In Texas, for a life sentence with parole, we must first serve forty years—if some can even survive that.

Make no mistake, getting off death row gave me a chance to have a future and to see change. However, instead of a quick death, I face a slow rot. This is a brutal place. It is hell! This experience drinks from your spirit until you become an empty shell.

Opportunities are limited. I hunt for them. I don't want anyone to believe that the Texas prison system is a great place with opportunities.

Published Author

Not long after *No Choirboy* was published, Nanon republished the books he wrote when he was on death row: *Still Surviving*, *The Darkest Hour: Stories and Interviews from Death Row*, and *The Ties That Bind Us*. He also wrote a children's book, *Peace People*. A textbook version of *The Darkest Hour* was coauthored with Dr. Betty Gilmore, a professor at Southern Methodist University. He continues to write.

Life in Prison

When I asked Nanon if he made friends in prison, or is close to his cellmate, he wrote back saying that, after he read this question, he shook his head.

> *With people going home, getting in trouble, or the administration constantly changing our cells, I have ten to fifteen different cellmates per year. I don't easily consider someone a friend. A friendship (at least a healthy one) should be formed with people who have like principles, views, morals, etc. I treat everyone with respect. I help to tutor and educate all who ask, but I consider only a few friends.*

Recently Nanon has found a little personal relief making jewelry in a craft shop.

It is reserved for those who have a clean disciplinary sheet for at least a year. I make all types of jewelry with my own tools and supplies. This is the only thing that has allowed me to escape the daily grind of prison. Shaping metal, soldering, and working with my hands is not easy work, but it is my *work.*

According to Nanon, his time spent on death row carries a stigma.

It carries a watchful eye, a sense of fear. Some cellmates look at my size and learn that I was on death row and refuse to be locked in a cell with me. Guards watch me like I am the exception. I don't fit the profile of someone who should be on death row, but they don't know about my conviction. They assume the worse; that I am a serial killer of some kind.

Over time people learn differently. Then I am embraced, admired, respected. Yet, that is constant work in an ever-shifting environment. I don't know how to update my life. My dreams may be altered, but I still have them.

I am strong. I am spirited. I believe in the goodness of people. I believe that most people desire to do good things. Justice, fairness, and equality are all subjective. I only know the extremes—the worst of all judgments. I don't believe justice exists, but I believe there are just people.

To learn more, please visit Nanon's Web site, www.nanonwilliams.com.

A Conversation with Bryan Stevenson

Bryan Stevenson, the executive director of the Equal Justice Initiative (EJI) and a participant in *No Choirboy*, talked with me about his clients Roy and Mark, and about the recent changes in the law for juvenile offenders. EJI is a nonprofit organization that represents people who could not otherwise afford strong legal counsel.

Bryan and his team of lawyers argued three important cases regarding juveniles before the Supreme Court that led to landmark rulings: *Graham v. Florida* (2010), *Miller v. Alabama* (2012), and *Jackson v. Hobbs* (2012). *Miller* and *Jackson* were argued together. These cases are described in greater detail at the end of this conversation.

Bryan's Clients, Roy and Mark

BRYAN: Roy has grown a good bit. He does reasonably well with his institutional history [behavioral record in prison]; he attends classes and works in various prison jobs. We're hopeful that he will get a reduced sentence now that mandatory life without parole for juveniles has been banned. Because we're still challenging his conviction, we will first complete that litigation before going back to the court for a new sentence. Roy will obviously have to do some more time. But if we succeed in getting a life *with* parole sentence, he will be parole-eligible very soon. That doesn't mean he will get parole, but I think he's excited and encouraged by the possibility of having the chance to get out.

SUSAN: What's the level of security at Roy's prison?

BRYAN: He's at a maximum-security prison because he still has a life without parole sentence. If you have that sentence, you have to be in a maximum-security prison. Since Mark's sentence is life *with* parole, he can be in a medium-security prison.

SUSAN: Tell me about Mark.

BRYAN: I've actually done a lot of work with Mark in the last several years. We spent time working on improving his institutional history and he's gotten a lot, lot better. He has gone several years with no disciplinaries.

In 2008, Mark was sent to a six-month program at the LifeTech Institute* that could have resulted in his release from prison. The institute is in a secure facility run by the parole board. Only a small percentage of people successfully complete the program and obtain release. When Mark was in the program, he had some day passes. One day I picked him up and took him to a restaurant. He was wearing street clothes. We went to McDonald's and he got a burger. Then we went to a Dairy Queen and he got a vanilla milkshake with whipped cream. He said he had been dreaming about that for years.

After three months at the program, Mark violated one of the center's rules. He didn't do anything illegal, but there are lots of technical requirements which, if violated, can get you sent back to prison. Not reporting to your officer on time, failing to notify someone of your whereabouts, missing class or an appointment. These "technical violations" are what keep most people in prison when they've been considered for parole.

In 2013, Mark was denied parole by the parole board. Although he remains incarcerated, he is still parole-eligible. He has another parole hearing in about three years. We're hoping that he will get released then.

*[The LifeTech Institute's Web site states: "The program trains parolees for successful reentry into the world of work and helps reduce Alabama prison overcrowding. . . . The LifeTech Institute teaches life skills and technical skills to help parolees make the transition from prison to society. Alabama Southern provides the education component of the program as well as statewide job placement services in coordination with business and industry. The Alabama Board of Pardons and Parole provides housing and other components of the parole transition center."]

SUSAN: Is he back in the same prison?

BRYAN: He's at a prison called Easterling. It's a medium-security facility and he's doing well. He's in the honor dorm. He's had no disciplinaries. He's not playing music but he's gotten very serious about his art and drawing. He's doing some remarkable artwork.

New Supreme Court Laws

BRYAN: In 2005, the Supreme Court struck down the death penalty for juvenile offenders (*Roper v. Simmons*). That opened up the constitutional landscape for conversations about how we sentence children in the criminal justice system.

After the Court's decision in *Roper*, all those people that I represented who were on death row for crimes they committed as children were relieved that they weren't going to be executed. But they weren't encouraged by sentences that required them to stay in prison until they die. Their death sentences were replaced with life in prison without parole, which in some ways is just another kind of death sentence.

During my conversations with juvenile clients, we decided to challenge death-in-prison sentences for children, whether it's death by execution or death by incarceration.

We started a campaign that focused on two categories of children who had been sentenced to life in prison without parole. One category was all children who had been fourteen years of age and younger. About a hundred kids who were thirteen and fourteen years old were sentenced to die in prison.

SUSAN: Did that include murder?
BRYAN: Yes. All children fourteen and younger included all crimes.

The second category had to do with children or juveniles who were convicted of crimes other than murder. There were about two hundred kids in that category. We went to the United States Supreme Court and argued the case. In 2010, the Court ruled that life without parole for children convicted of non-homicide crimes was unconstitutional.

That case (*Graham v. Florida*) meant that all people who had been sentenced to life without parole for crimes committed for non-homicide offenses would be resentenced to a term that would give them "a meaningful possibility of release." No juvenile can be sentenced to die in prison for a non-homicide crime.

We have been working on getting people eligible for relief resentences ever since. A lot of them have been released, which has been great. There are only a handful of states that have non-homicide life without parole sentences. Most of the cases were in Florida and Louisiana. Some were in Oklahoma, Virginia, and California.

After that case, we went back to the Court and made

arguments about life without parole for children convicted of all crimes, including murder. In 2012, the Court
agreed to take up that issue. In *Miller v. Alabama*, the Court
ruled that mandatory life without parole sentences, even
for murder, is unconstitutional. Kids who had a mandatory sentence of life without parole for murder are now
entitled to relief as well.

SUSAN: Can you explain *mandatory*?
BRYAN: *Mandatory* means that the judge had no discretion
or choice when imposing a life without parole sentence.
By finding the person guilty of first-degree murder, capital
murder, the judge *must* impose a life without parole. There
are nearly 3,000 people serving life without parole for
crimes they committed as juveniles. About 2,400 to 2,500
of those 3,000 cases are there because their sentence was
mandatory.

SUSAN: What happens if the sentence is discretionary?
BRYAN: If it's discretionary, judges have a choice. They
can sentence a juvenile to something less harsh. Judges are
not blocked from imposing a life without parole sentence
after full consideration of age and other relevant circumstances. The Supreme Court's decision doesn't specifically,
expressly prohibit life without parole for juvenile offenders,
but it should be "uncommon."
    After *Miller* came down, we started filing cases on

behalf of lots of people who had been sentenced to life without parole in a mandatory proceeding. Those cases are now pending. Some states have tried to prevent us from applying the *Miller* decision retroactively to people who have already been convicted and sentenced. There is some chance that people like Roy will be prevented from getting relief based on this retroactivity question. But a bunch of states have already ruled that they think that the case ruling is fully retroactive, and we continuing to operate assuming that it is.

SUSAN: How do these laws relate specifically to Roy?
BRYAN: Roy is now entitled to a new sentencing hearing.

SUSAN: But he would not automatically be entitled to parole?
BRYAN: That's right. And we still have to persuade the sentencer that life *with* parole is a more appropriate sentence for Roy than life without parole.

SUSAN: Was Roy's sentence mandatory?
BRYAN: It was. At the time of his sentencing, the judge had no discretion to sentence Roy to something less extreme than life imprisonment without parole. With the new law in place, he is now entitled to relief. The court has the discretion to sentence him to life with parole or life without parole, which is not something he had previously. But the

Court doesn't *have* to give him life with parole. That's the kicker.

New Campaigns

BRYAN: We have two new campaigns. The first one is to create a minimum age when a child can be tried as an adult. There are some states that have no such minimum age. That means eight, nine, ten, and eleven-year-olds can be tried as an adult. We want to change that.

The second campaign is to end the incarceration, the housing of children, in adult jails and prisons. There are about 10,000 kids on any given day in an adult jail or an adult prison. These children are at greater risk of sexual assault and violence. They are at greater risk of suicide. And so we're trying to get the Court to ban the incarceration of children with adults—even if they are prosecuted as adults.

Race

BRYAN: I think we do a poor job talking about race in this country, and we don't have a very good understanding of racial history. At EJI, we decided to find a sensible way to talk about race and the legacy of racial history. We've created a project that looks at our racial history.

I think we have to understand the trauma, the difficulty, the unfairness, the subordination, and the injustice created by racial injustice to really have an informed conversation about race. We have to acknowledge and understand where myths about black inferiority come from. So we want to mark and identify the slave trading sites in this country. By talking about this history, we want to raise consciousness about the history and the legacy of slavery.

We're developing educational tools for young kids and for adults. We've produced a calendar that addresses racial inequality. It's not a celebratory calendar that emphasizes achievements. It emphasizes times that were difficult and challenging and unfair.

We also have to talk about post-slavery realities, and about the era of terror for people of color. For African Americans, from the end of Reconstruction in the 1870s until World War II, racial terror was the defining reality of their lives. They had to worry about lynchings, convict leasing, and hate crimes.

SUSAN: Convict leasing?
BRYAN: Convict leasing took place in states like Alabama, Mississippi, and Georgia. They made criminal offenses of such things as being out past curfew, loitering, or getting a job without a former slave master's permission. These laws were directed at former slaves. They would arrest people for violating made-up "crimes," convict them, and then lease the convicted people to private companies who would pay the state for what amounted to slave labor.

Doug Blackman, the journalist, wrote a book called

Slavery by Another Name, where convict leasing was characterized as the re-enslavement of black Americans. This took place from the end of the nineteenth century to the 1930s. It was a terrifying institution that people of color had to confront. Along with lynching and racial violence and bombings, a generation of people grew up with terrorism as the defining feature of their lives. We need to talk more about the Jim Crow era, the segregation era, the apartheid era.

We are over-prosecuting people of color. We have racial profiling. Stop and frisk. We look at people through the lens of race. The presumptions of criminality and dangerousness and guilt assigned to black and brown men and boys have a legacy that's rooted in slavery. It has continued for centuries.

My thesis is that we cannot recover from decades of human rights violations like these without committing ourselves to a process of truth and reconciliation, as they have done in South Africa. They are doing it in Rwanda following the genocide. We've got to create space for people to tell the truth about what they've experienced when they were the victims of systemic, constant, intense discrimination and bias. And because we haven't done that in this country, I don't believe we have become reconciled to our history. We still have conflicts and tensions when it comes to race. Our project is aimed at getting people to talk about it.

To learn more about this project and about the Equal Justice Initiative, visit www.eji.org/racepoverty/racialinjustice.

Most Recent Laws For Juveniles

In 2009, Equal Justice Initiative attorneys went to the Supreme Court to fight for a constitutional ban to end death-in-prison sentences on children. According to the report put out by EJI, *All Children Are Children: Challenging Abusive Punishment of Juveniles*, EJI attorneys argued the following cases before the Supreme Court:

Graham v. Florida, 2010

THE CASE:

Terrance Jamar Graham was sixteen when he and two friends tried to rob a barbecue restaurant in Florida. He was charged as an adult for armed burglary, assault, and attempted robbery. He pleaded guilty, his charge was accepted, and he was paroled. Six months later he was arrested again for home invasion robbery. This put him in violation of his parole. He was sentenced to life in prison without parole.

THE SUPREME COURT RULING:

In *Graham v. Florida*, the Supreme Court agreed that juvenile offenders cannot be sentenced to life in prison without parole for non-homicide cases. Justice Anthony Kennedy wrote for the majority opinion of the court. "The Constitution prohibits the imposition of a life without parole sentence on a juvenile offender who did not commit homicide. A State need not guarantee the offender eventual release, but if it imposes a sentence of life, it must provide him or her with some realistic opportunity to obtain release before the end of that term."

Miller v. Alabama, 2012 & *Jackson v. Hobbs,* 2012

THE CASES:

Evan Miller, a fourteen-year-old Alabamian, was convicted of murder after he and another boy beat and robbed a neighbor who sold them drugs. They tried to conceal evidence by setting fire to the neighbor's trailer. The neighbor died of smoke inhalation. Miller was given a life sentence with no parole.

Kuntrell Jackson from Arkansas was also fourteen when he and two friends planned to rob a video store. Kuntrell was outside when one of the kids shot the store clerk. Jackson was caught and charged as an adult and sentenced to life in prison without parole.

THE SUPREME COURT RULING:

Bryan Stevenson and EJI lawyers argued that these two cases in which fourteen-year-old children had been sentenced to die in prison after being convicted of homicide crimes was cruel and unusual and violated the Eighth Amendment. The majority of the Court agreed with him.

Justice Elena Kagan delivered the majority opinion. "Mandatory life without parole for those under age of 18 at the time of their crime violates the 8th Amendment's prohibition on cruel and unusual punishment. Mandatory life without parole for a juvenile precludes consideration of his chronological age and its hallmark features—among them, immaturity, impetuosity, and failure to appreciate risks and consequences." Justice Kagan added, "It prevents taking into account the family and home environment that surrounds him—and from which he cannot usually extricate himself—no matter how brutal or dysfunctional."

An interview with the author Susan Kuklin

What inspired you to tackle this topic?

A number of years ago, I wrote a book about human rights called *Irresistible Spirit: Conversations with Human Rights Activists*. Capital punishment was an issue much talked about by American human rights workers. In fact, it became a chapter in the book. Later, Ursula Bentele, a friend who works on legal issues regarding national and international capital punishment, encouraged me to join her at various lectures and symposiums. It was because of Ursula that I first heard lectures by Bryan Stevenson and Sister Helen Prejean (the author of *Dead Man Walking*). They were inspiring. I knew that I had to do something to bring this issue to young adults. Hence the book.

What was the most difficult part of writing this book?

The most difficult part of writing the book was deciding what information to put in and what to leave out. The subject is huge. And the more I learned, the more the themes and ideas evolved. *No Choirboy* was written and rewritten many times.

As a nonfiction author, I cannot resist facts. To research the book, I gathered interesting tidbits of legal and historical information. My first draft included boxed legal information throughout the interviews. My second draft included major U.S. law and a (sort of) brief history of capital punishment. My editor and I agreed that what the inmates revealed about life in prison was the most interesting and important part of the book. We did not want to turn this into the "ultimate YA textbook" on capital punishment and juvenile justice. I rewrote the book once again, taking out the additional material and simply letting the inmates speak for themselves. Some of the deleted information can be found on my Web site, www.susankuklin.com.

Did you expect me to say the most difficult part was going to prisons and working with the inmates? Although it was an emotional experience, it was also exhilarating and, in some way, life affirming. Although I never forgot that the inmates committed terrible crimes, they were warm, introspective, and had much they wanted to share.

What is the most valuable thing you learned during the research/writing process for *No Choirboy*?

I learned that one's worst act—though unforgivable—is not the sum total of a human being. I learned that violence

begets violence. I learned that if we are to consider ourselves a just society, we need to look closer at the way we
treat those we call "the worst of the worst." I learned that
people are very, very complicated.

How did you choose the specific people whose stories you tell in the book?

I wanted to interview articulate, insightful inmates who
were under eighteen when they committed their crimes.
But first I had to know what I was talking about. I attended
a seminar with Ursula Bentele at Brooklyn Law School.
There, I realized I needed to know much more. I called
Bryan Stevenson, a law professor at New York University
Law School, and asked if I could audit his class, Capital
Punishment Law and Litigation. He agreed, and helped
me find people to interview. Two of the inmates are Bryan's clients. Bryan also introduced me to the director of
the Texas Defender Service. This is a nonprofit group of
lawyers who handle the appeals for indigent prisoners on
death row. One person led to another. And another. And
another.

Do you keep in touch with any of the inmates or family members you met while research-ing the book?

Yes. I continue to write to and receive letters from Roy
and Nanon. I wish I could write another book using their

letters. Both cry out for intellectual stimulation. They ask and discuss big questions. I hear their mood swings, their yearnings. Reading and writing keep them sane.

Could you please explain the significance of the book's title?

Chapter three, "Look at Me," is about Nanon M. Williams. When I interviewed him, he was still on death row in Texas even though the law had changed. (He is currently in a maximum-security prison.) At one point Nanon said, "I know I'm no choirboy, but I don't deserve this!" That line summed up what I was trying to say in the book.

Have any of the inmates in the book been affected by the Supreme Court ruling that declared the death penalty unconstitutional for offenders under eighteen?

All but one, Mark, were affected in some way by the Supreme Court ruling. Bryan Stevenson is currently working on new appeals for Roy. He had already successfully sought to reduce Roy's death sentence to life without parole. Now that the new ruling has come out, he is trying to reduce it again to a life sentence *with* the possibility of parole.

Nanon, as mentioned, was on death row at the time of the ruling. He is now in a maximum security prison hoping for a new trial. The death penalty did not apply to Mark because he was too young at the time of the crime.

Napoleon, unfortunately, did not benefit from the new ruling. His lawyers begged the court and the governor to stay his execution until the Supreme Court ruling. They did not wait.

What did you learn about the criminal justice system?

Oh, I don't know where to begin. By taking the law school courses, I learned how complex our system is, especially the appeals system. I learned that a great number of people in our prisons grew up in an atmosphere of violence, acted violently, and continue to spend the rest of their lives isolated in an extremely violent society. Although I still believe that people must be held accountable for horrific acts, I was shocked and saddened by the some of their treatment by both guards and other inmates. Solitary confinement seems downright medieval in its cruelty.

GLOSSARY

(Some of the words listed here are frequently used legal terms and may not appear in the text.)

AGGRAVATION An act or circumstance that increases the gravity of a crime but is not part of the crime itself (for example, threatening to beat up a kidnap victim).

APPEAL The process of seeking review of one's case in a higher (or appellate) court following the decision of a lower court.

APPELLATE COURT A court that reviews cases from a lower court. The U.S. Supreme Court is the highest appellate court in the country.

ARRAIGNMENT The first step of a criminal proceeding. The accused person is brought before a judge and told the charges against him. At this time, the accused person enters a plea, guilty or not guilty.

BAIL Security paid for the release of an arrested person that is held as a guarantee that the person will appear for trial.

BRIEF A written document specifying the facts, law, and arguments supporting the party's position on the case.

BROWN V. BOARD OF EDUCATION The landmark Supreme Court case that abolished legal segregation in schools in 1954.

COMMUTE To reduce a sentence, especially a death sentence, to one that is less severe.

DA (DISTRICT ATTORNEY) A prosecuting attorney who represents the state during a trial.

EXCLUSIONARY RULE   A rule that forbids the use of illegally obtained evidence during a trial. For example, information obtained from an illegal search is prohibited.

EXCULPATORY   Supporting the contention that the defendant is not guilty.

EXONERATE   To clear of all blame.

EXTRADITE   To deliver a person arrested for a crime in another state or country to the place where the crime was committed.

FELONY   A category of crimes considered more serious than lesser crimes, which are known as misdemeanors.

FELONY MURDER   The participation in a felony (other than murder) that leads to a death, typically considered as blameworthy as first-degree murder.

HABEAS   Short for the Latin habeas corpus, which means "you have the body." A habeas proceeding determines whether a person in custody has been confined according to constitutional rules.

HEARING   A legal proceeding about a specific subject.

HEARSAY   Statements by parties who are not present in the courtroom. Such statements are generally not allowed into evidence, although there are many exceptions to this rule.

INCULPATORY   Tending to establish guilt.

MATERIAL   Important to the issues in a case, necessary.

MIRANDA RULE   A legal statement that must be promptly read by an arresting officer when a suspect is taken into custody in order for statements or evidence gathered from the accused to be admissible in court. It includes the information that a suspect has the right to remain silent, that anything the person does say may be used against him in court, that he has a right to an attorney, and that if he cannot afford an attorney, one will be appointed for him. This warning came into effect in 1966 as a result of the U.S. Supreme Court case *Miranda v. Arizona.*

MITIGATING CIRCUMSTANCES   Experiences or situations that can reduce the convicted defendant's penalty, such as being a first offender or having had a very hard life.

PAROLE   The early release of a prisoner who has served part of his sentence. He serves the rest of his term under parole supervision.

PLEA BARGAIN An agreement, subject to court approval, by a defendant to plead guilty to a lesser charge.

REMAND To send back. A case from a higher court may be remanded to a lower court for a new hearing or trial.

REVERSE To change or turn aside a lower court's decision.

STATE'S EVIDENCE In return for immunity or a lesser sentence, a participant in a crime agrees to testify against other participants.

STAY To stop or postpone a judicial proceeding (for example, to stay an execution).

FURTHER READING

FICTION BOOKS

CAPOTE, TRUMAN. *In Cold Blood.* Modern Library, New York, reissue.

DREISER, THEODORE. *An American Tragedy.* Signet Classics, New York, 2000 reissue.

LEE, HARPER. *To Kill a Mockingbird.* HarperCollins 40th anniversary edition, New York, 1999.

MYERS, WALTER DEAN. *Monster.* HarperCollins, New York, 2001.

NONFICTION BOOKS

CARTER, DAN T. *Scottsboro: A Tragedy of the American South.* Louisiana State University Press, Baton Rouge, 1969.

JENKINS, BILL. *What to Do When the Police Leave: A Guide to the First Days of Traumatic Loss,* third ed. WBJ Press, Chicago, 2001.

LIFTON, ROBERT JAY, AND GREG MITCHELL. *Who Owns Death? Capital Punishment, the American Conscience, and the End of Executions.* Perennial paperback, HarperCollins, New York, 2000.

PREJEAN, HELEN. *Dead Man Walking: An Eyewitness Account of the Death Penalty in the United States.* Vintage Books, New York, 1994.

SOLOTAROFF, IVAN. *The Last Face You'll Ever See: The Private Life of the American Death Penalty.* Perennial paperback, HarperCollins, New York, 2001.

WILLIAMS, NANON MCKEWN. *The Darkest Hour.* Breakout Publishing Company, Gardena, California, 2002.

———. *Still Surviving.* Breakout Publishing Company, Gardena, California, 2003.

———. *The Ties That Bind Us.* Breakout Publishing Company, Gardena, California, 2001.

ZEHR, HOWARD. *Doing Life: Reflections of Men and Women Serving Life Sentences.* Good Books, Intercourse, Pennsylvania, 1996.

WEB SITES

American Bar Association:
www.abanet.org

Amnesty International USA:
www.amnestyusa.org

Court TV's Crime Library:
www.crimelibrary.com

Death Penalty Information Center:
www.deathpenaltyinfo.org

Death Penalty, Michigan State University (a high school death
penalty curriculum):
www.deathpenaltyinfo.msu.edu/intro.htm

Equal Justice Initiative of Alabama:
www.eji.org

Famous American Trials: The Scottsboro Boys:
www.law.umkc.edu

Human Rights Watch:
http://hrw.org

Innocence Project Northwest:
www.law.washington.edu/ipnw/

Murder Victims' Families Against the Death Penalty:
www.mvfr.org

Murder Victims' Families for Human Rights:
www.murdervictimsfamilies.org

Texas Defender Service:
www.texasdefender.org

Will's World (dedicated to the memory of William Benjamin Jenkins):
www.willsworld.com

NOTES

Most of the photographs are by the author. Additional photographs and drawings are courtesy of the participants in the book.

CHAPTER ONE
I Was a Teenager on Death Row

Information about Roy's case is from the "State's Brief and Argument on Petition for a Writ of Certiorari to the Alabama Court of Criminal Appeals" (93-1270), the "Brief of Appellant" by Bryan A. Stevenson and J. Drew Colfax, No. 1980810, and interviews with lawyers Aaryn M. Urell and Bryan Stevenson.

CHAPTER THREE
Look at Me

The decision in the United States Supreme Court case *Roper v. Simmons*, 543 U.S. 511 (2005) states that the eighth and fourteenth amendments prohibit the execution of offenders who were under the age of eighteen when their crimes were committed.

This chapter incorporates quotes from *Still Surviving* by Nanon McKewn Williams (Breakout Publishing Co., 2003).

CHAPTER FOUR
Hate Is a Killer

Additional information about this case is from Walter Long's clemency petition.

Napoleon Beazley's last words were quoted in the following newspaper article: "Killer of Judge's Father Executed," by Paul Duggan (*Washington Post*, May 29, 2002).

CHAPTER SIX
Dying for Legal Assistance

The case Bryan Stevenson refers to is *Nelson v. Campbell*, 541 U.S. 637 (2004). The Court ruled that the civil rights statute, rather than habeas corpus, was an appropriate way to challenge the means of execution and therefore a stay should be granted.

GLOSSARY

These definitions were researched via the *Gilbert Law Dictionary*, Harcourt Brace Legal and Professional Publications, Inc., 1997; *The Free Dictionary (online)*, by Farlex; as well as with the keen eyes of Ursula Bentele, Bailey Kuklin, and Bryan Stevenson.

INDEX

(Page numbers in *italic* refer to illustrations.)